AMERICAN
WAR LIBRARY
★ ★ ★ ★

★ The Cold War ★

CONTAINING THE COMMUNISTS: AMERICA'S FOREIGN ENTANGLEMENTS

by Jennifer Keeley

LUCENT
BOOKS®

THOMSON
★
™
GALE

San Diego • Detroit • New York • San Francisco • Cleveland • New Haven, Conn. • Waterville, Maine • London • Munich

On cover: Battle-weary American troops withdraw from Yong San in Korea on September 14, 1950.

© 2003 by Lucent Books. Lucent Books is an imprint of The Gale Group, Inc., a division of Thomson Learning, Inc.

Lucent Books® and Thomson Learning™ are trademarks used herein under license.

For more information, contact
Lucent Books
27500 Drake Rd.
Farmington Hills, MI 48331-3535
Or you can visit our Internet site at http://www.gale.com

LIBRARY OF CONGRESS CATALOGING-IN-PUBLICATION DATA

Keeley, Jennifer, 1974–.
    Containing the Communists: America's foreign entanglements / by Jennifer Keeley.
      v. cm. — (American war library. Cold War series)
Includes bibliographical references and index.
Contents: Washington's warnings—Containing Communism—Korea, containing Communism in Asia—Egypt, Arab Nationalism versus containment—Cuba—Vietnam—Angola—Nicaragua and the Iran-Contra Affair.
    ISBN 1-59018-225-1
    1. United States—Foreign relations—1945–1989—Juvenile literature.
2. United States—Foreign relations—Communist countries—Juvenile literature.
3. Communist countries—Foreign relations—United States—Juvenile literature.
4. Cold War—Diplomatic history—Juvenile literature. [1. United States—Foreign relations—1945–1989. 2. Communism. 3. United States—History—1945–1989. 4. Cold War.] I. Title. II. Series.
    E744 .K25 2003
    327.73'009'045—dc21
                                    2002013621

Printed in the United States of America

☆ Contents ☆

A Nation Forged by War

The United States, like many nations, was forged and defined by war. Despite Benjamin Franklin's opinion that "There never was a good war or a bad peace," the United States owes its very existence to the War of Independence, one to which Franklin wholeheartedly subscribed. The country forged by war in 1776 was tempered and made stronger by the Civil War in the 1860s.

The Texas Revolution, the Mexican-American War, and the Spanish-American War expanded the country's borders and gave it overseas possessions. These wars made the United States a world power, but this status came with a price, as the nation became a key but reluctant player in both World War I and World War II.

Each successive war further defined the country's role on the world stage. Following World War II, U.S. foreign policy redefined itself to focus on the role of defender, not only of the freedom of its own citizens but also of the freedom of people everywhere. During the Cold War that followed World War II until the collapse of the Soviet Union, defending the world meant fighting communism. This goal, manifested in the Korean and Vietnam conflicts, proved elusive and soured the American public on its achievability. As the United States emerged as the world's sole superpower, American foreign policy has been guided less by national interest and more on protecting international human rights. But as involvement in Somalia and Kosovo proves, this goal has been equally elusive.

As a result, the country's view of itself changed. Bolstered by victories in World Wars I and II, Americans first relished the role of protector. But, as war followed war in a seemingly endless procession, Americans began to doubt their leaders, their motives, and themselves. The Vietnam War especially caused people to question the validity of sending young people to die in places where they were not particularly wanted and for people who did not seem especially grateful.

While the most obvious changes brought about by America's wars have been geopolitical in nature, many other aspects of society have been touched. War often does not bring about change directly but acts instead like the catalyst in a chemical reaction, accelerating changes already in progress.

Some of these changes have been societal. The role of women in the United States had been slowly changing, but World War II put thousands into the workforce and into uniform. They might have gone back to being housewives after the war, but equality, once experienced, would not be forgotten.

Likewise, wars have accelerated technological change. The necessity for faster airplanes and a more destructive bomb led to the development of jet planes and nuclear energy. Artificial fibers developed for parachutes in the 1940s were used in the clothing of the 1950s.

Lucent Books' American War Library covers key wars in the development of the nation. Each war is covered in several volumes to allow for more detail, context, and to provide volumes on often neglected subjects, such as the kamikazes of World War II or weapons used in the Civil War. As with all Lucent Books, notes, annotated bibliographies, and appendixes such as glossaries give students a launching point for further research. In addition, sidebars and archival photographs enhance the text. Together, each volume in the American War Library will aid students in understanding how America's wars have shaped and changed its politics, economics, and society.

Washington's Warnings

I n his farewell address to the nation in 1796, President George Washington warned future American governments not "to entangle our peace and prosperity" with that of other nations. His successors typically heeded this advice, and, as a result, the United States played a very limited role in world affairs in the eighteenth and nineteenth centuries. However, the twentieth century brought with it incredible advances in technology that made contact with the rest of the world both easier and more likely. In addition, the early part of the century saw two consecutive wars that thrust the United States into the world arena.

At the end of the Second World War, the United States emerged as one of two world superpowers, and its leaders quickly recognized the influence they could have around the globe. In October 1944 President Franklin D. Roosevelt declared, "there is literally no question, political or military, in which the United States is not interested."[1] Suddenly, a nation that had shied away from entangling itself in foreign affairs was announcing its desire to play a more active role in global politics.

However, there was another superpower, the Soviet Union [Union of Soviet Socialist Republics, or USSR], and its leaders had similar aspirations. "The USSR is now one of the mightiest countries in the world," Soviet foreign minister Vyacheslav Molotov stated in 1946. "One cannot decide now *any* serious problems of international relations without the USSR."[2] With both superpowers laying claim to a say in all events around the globe, as author P.M.H. Bell points out in *The World Since 1945: An International History*, "the interests of the two states would be almost certain to conflict at some point and at some time."[3] In other words, there was bound to be trouble.

Trouble was even more likely between the United States and the USSR because they had completely different societies

British Prime Minister Winston Churchill (left), President Franklin D. Roosevelt (center), and Soviet premier Joseph Stalin gather at Yalta in 1945 to discuss the post-WWII fate of Europe.

based on two different political and economic systems. The United States political system is often referred to as a democracy (it is actually a democratic republic) because citizens elect people to represent them in their local, state, and federal governments. Its economy is based on the principles of capitalism in which property, goods, and the means of producing them can be privately owned. The Soviet Union, on the other hand, had a Communist economic and political system based on the theories of Karl Marx and Vladimir Ilyich Lenin, in which the laborers rise up and overthrow capitalism and then establish a society where all goods and property are communally owned.

Since communism requires the destruction of capitalism, these two nations were in ideological opposition to each other. To make matters worse, each superpower believed the other had plans to destroy its "way of life" and take over the world. The result was a great deal of hostility and paranoia between two powerful nations, which threatened but never developed into an outright military confrontation. This period of history, in which the United States and the USSR fought an intense ideological battle to defend and expand their respective political and economic systems is called the Cold War.

The Soviets and the United States never quarreled directly with each other during this time. They simply did so under the cover of other nations, which became pawns in the struggle between the two superpowers. When either the USSR or the United States identified a nation that it might influence to further its own Cold War foreign policy goals, each superpower attempted to bring a supportive regime to power in that nation. In the case of the United States, the overriding goal was to stop the spread of communism, and U.S. officials willingly committed U.S. resources around the globe in service of this cause. As a result, the United States became politically, economically, and/or militarily "entangled" in the affairs of numerous nations throughout the Cold War, and this shaped their histories as well as the history of the world.

Chapter 1

Containing Communism

The willingness of the United States to become entangled in the domestic affairs of other nations was a new development in the years following World War II. This shift in foreign policy was precipitated by a series of events that occurred in the latter years of the war and immediately following it. During this time, the United States went from a somewhat strained alliance with the Communist government of the Soviet Union to dedicating its military forces to stop the spread of communism across the globe.

The Fear of Appeasement

In the years leading up to World War II, the British and French governments were the two most powerful European nations and therefore the two nations strong enough to oppose the expansionist policies of Adolf Hitler and Nazi Germany. However, time and again these two powerful nations gave in to Hitler's territorial demands because they wished to avoid

war. This policy of giving Hitler whatever he wanted in an attempt to prevent another European war came to be known as appeasement.

The British and French leaders who practiced appeasement truly believed it was the road to peace, but numerous politicians, diplomats, and historians have since blamed the extent of World War II on the policy of appeasement practiced in the years preceding it. They argue that Hitler and the Nazis could have been easily stopped in these early stages but were instead given more territory, more resources, and more manpower through the appeasement policies of the British and French. As a result, when war broke out in 1939, France, Great Britain, and eventually the world faced a Germany made all the more powerful by the conciliations made in these early years.

Governments around the globe took note of what appeasement in the name of preserving peace had wrought, and vowed never to allow a government with aggressive expansionist policies to devastate Europe again. Emerging from the war as one of two world superpowers and therefore with a sense of responsibility for world affairs, the United States heeded this advice.

Security Versus Expansion

One man's quest for his nation's security can be construed by other nations as aggressive expansion, and the man who most wanted security at the end of World War II was Joseph Stalin, the leader of the Soviet Union. In roughly twenty-five years, the USSR had been attacked twice by Germany. Both times, the Germans had come through Poland. The Soviet leader was determined that Russia should never again be so easily attacked from the west. Thus, as the tide of the war turned, he worked to secure his nation in the future by creating a buffer zone between Western Europe and the USSR.

Over the course of the war, Stalin gained control over the Baltic States of Latvia, Estonia, and Lithuania and made them part of the Soviet Union. As the war drew to a close, he also wanted control over the eastern European nations of Poland, Czechoslovakia, Hungary, Romania, and Bulgaria. In his vision, these nations would become Soviet satellites—separate nations with their own governments that would be completely loyal to the wishes of Moscow (the seat of the Soviet

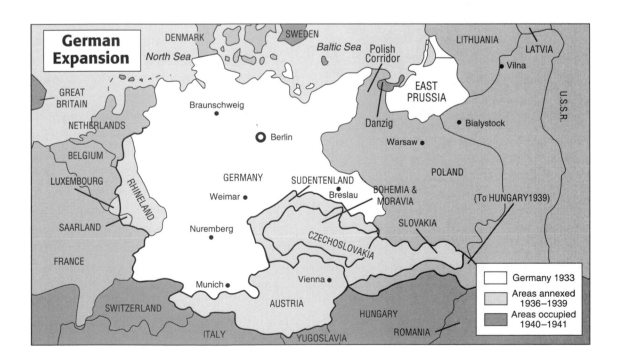

Joseph Stalin, pictured here during a 1935 speech, claimed much of Eastern Europe for the USSR following WWII.

government). By controlling these states, Stalin hoped both to shield Russia from any attacks that might be launched by western European nations and to expand the sphere of Soviet (and thus Communist) influence in the world.

Therefore, as the Soviets pushed back the Germans in Eastern Europe, they also made a play for control. The Nazis had occupied and administered these lands, and as they fled, war-torn nations were left behind with no government. The Soviets quickly found ways to seize power through force and deception, and by 1947 the USSR controlled the Communist governments of Poland, Rumania, and Hungary.

Stalin claimed the Soviet takeover of eastern European nations was for defensive purposes. He argued that these nations provided a "buffer zone" between the USSR and Western Europe, which safeguarded the Soviet Union from any future attacks by the capitalist nations of the West. However, this expansion of the Soviet Union made some world leaders uneasy, and they wondered whether Stalin was really seeking security or whether he, like Hitler before him, was bent on unlimited conquest.

Kennan's Long Telegram

For American officials wondering what the Soviets were thinking, the words of George F. Kennan, a senior diplomat who had been in Moscow since the 1930s, seemed to offer an answer. In February 1946 Kennan wrote what came to be called the "long telegram" in response to a fairly routine inquiry by the State Department.

The long telegram was aptly named, as it contained more than eight thousand words and gave a detailed explanation of Soviet history, ideology, territorial ambitions, and political aspirations. Kennan concluded the Soviets were "a political force committed fanatically to the belief that with [the] US there can be no permanent *modus vivendi* [truce], that it is desirable and necessary that the internal harmony of our society be disrupted, our traditional way of life be destroyed, the international authority of our state be broken, if Soviet power is to be secure."[4] In other words, in Kennan's opinion, one of the most powerful nations in the world was out to get the United States.

As for a course of action, Kennan's telegram pointed out that Soviet power was "highly sensitive to logic of force. For this reason it can easily withdraw—and usually does—when strong resistance is encountered at any point." Thus, all the United States had to do was make certain it had "sufficient force" and "make clear [its] readiness to use it." If the government

would take these steps, this force rarely would have to be used, since the Soviets would back down before they engaged in any "prestige-engaging showdowns."[5]

Kennan's telegram provided U.S. officials with a thoughtful, seemingly knowledgeable explanation of Soviet motives and behaviors where no explanation had existed before. Over time, it became a bible for U.S. officials attempting to understand the psyche of the Soviets and thereby predict or influence Soviet actions.

The Iron Curtain

Roughly two weeks after Kennan's telegram to the State Department, British prime minister Winston Churchill voiced his concerns regarding Soviet expansion in a speech at Westminster College

Communism in the 1950s

UNION OF SOVIET SOCIALIST REPUBLICS

EG
HUNGARY
ROMANIA
BULGARIA
YU.
ALBANIA

MONGOLIA

NORTH KOREA

Pacific Ocean

PEOPLE'S REPUBLIC OF CHINA

SOUTH KOREA

☐ Communist countries

in Fulton, Missouri. He told listeners, "I do not believe that Soviet Russia desires war. What they desire is the fruits of war and the indefinite expansion of their power and doctrines." Churchill warned, "Nobody knows what Soviet Russia . . . intends to do in the immediate future, or what are the limits, if any, to their expansive and proselytizing tendencies."[6]

In Churchill's opinion, an "iron curtain" had descended upon Eastern Europe. Behind this curtain, the people under Soviet control lived under "police governments." It was the duty of the "English-speaking" nations to stand as a bulwark against further Soviet expansion, for, in Churchill's words, "there is nothing they admire so much as strength, and there is nothing for which they have less respect than for weakness."[7] Churchill counseled against appeasing Stalin in the way Hitler had been in the years prior to World War II, and urged the United States and its allies to be strong and start standing up to the Soviets.

The Domino Theory Emerges

By August 1946 the USSR had control of the Baltic states and had successfully installed "people's democracies," or puppet governments loyal to Moscow, in Poland, Romania, and Hungary. The voices of Kennan and Churchill were joined by a growing chorus of U.S. officials who had begun to question Soviet expansion.

A decisive shift in U.S. foreign policy had already begun and was further ad-

vanced by the situation in Greece in February 1947. The Greek government was fighting a bloody civil war against Communist guerillas supported by Yugoslavia. The British had been providing the Greeks with financial and military support, but in late February 1947 the British were facing a severe financial crisis. Since they could no longer afford to fund the Greek government's cause, the British appealed to the United States to assume the task in order to stop the Communists from gaining power in Greece.

The United States accepted the responsibility. This decision was based, in part, on a line of thinking that would later be dubbed the domino theory by President Harry S. Truman's successor, President Dwight D. Eisenhower. In a 1954 press conference, Eisenhower explained this falling domino principle: "You have a row of dominoes set up, you knock over the first one, and what will happen to the last one is the certainty that it will go over very quickly."[8] When this principle is applied to politics, countries are like dominoes, and once one domino "falls" to communism, it could knock over its neighbors causing them to fall—a chain reaction. In addition, the chain reaction picks up speed and momentum as it goes along, so while the first domino may fall over slowly, the last could go very quickly. It is therefore better to stop the first domino from ever falling rather than risk the chance that the last would go over so quickly it could not be stopped.

Stalin's Response to Churchill's "Iron Curtain" Speech

The following is an excerpt from an interview with Stalin that appeared in the Soviet state newspaper, *Pravda*, on March 14, 1946, shortly after Churchill's "iron curtain" speech. The article was translated from Russian and can be found at www.cnn.com.

Question: Could Mr. Churchill's speech be considered as a harm to the progress of peace and security?

Answer: Absolutely, yes. As a matter of fact Mr. Churchill is standing now in the position of a warmonger. And here Mr. Churchill is not alone—he has many friends not only in England but also in the United States. It ought to be mentioned that in this matter Mr. Churchill and his friends strikingly resemble Hitler and his friends. Hitler started the process of unleashing war from the proclamation of a racist theory, according to which only the German-speaking people are a worthy nation. Mr. Churchill is starting his process of unleashing war also from a racist theory, stating that only the English-speaking countries are worthy nations, destined to manage the fate of the world. German racist theory led Hitler and his friends to the conclusion that Germans, as the only worthy nation, should rule the other nations. English racist theory leads Mr. Churchill and his friends into the following conclusion: that English-speaking countries, as the only worthy nations, should govern the other nations of the world.

As a matter of fact, Mr. Churchill and his friends in England and in the United States are presenting the non-English-speaking nations with something like an ultimatum: either voluntarily agree to our rule, and everything will be all right, or a war is unavoidable. . . .

Undoubtedly, Mr. Churchill's aim is war, a war with the U.S.S.R.

British Prime Minister Winston Churchill coined the term "iron curtain" to describe Stalin's Soviet regime in Eastern Europe.

The Truman Doctrine

Perhaps one of the most influential addresses in the twentieth century, President Harry Truman's "Truman Doctrine" was unveiled during his March 12, 1947, address to a joint session of Congress. The speech in its entirety can be found at www.luminet.net.

At the present moment in world history nearly every nation must choose between alternative ways of life. The choice is too often not a free one.

One way of life is based upon the will of the majority, and is distinguished by free institutions, representative government, free elections, guarantees of individual liberty, freedom of speech and religion, and freedom from political oppression.

The second way of life is based upon the will of a minority forcibly imposed upon the majority. It relies upon terror and oppression, a controlled press and radio, fixed elections, and the suppression of personal freedoms.

I believe that it must be the policy of the United States to support free peoples who are resisting attempted subjugation by armed minorities or by outside pressures.

I believe that we must assist free peoples to work out their own destinies in their own way.

I believe that our help should be primarily through economic and financial aid which is essential to economic stability and orderly political processes.

In the specific case of Greece, President Truman argued that if this first domino "fell," all of Europe, the Middle East, and Asia potentially could follow. He told leading members of Congress:

If Greece should dissolve into civil war it is altogether probable that it would emerge as a communist state under Soviet control. Turkey would be surrounded and the Turkish situation . . . would in turn become still more critical. Soviet domination might thus extend over the entire Middle East to the borders of India. The effect of this upon Hungary, Austria, Italy and France cannot be overestimated. It is not alarmist to say that we are faced with the first crisis of a series which might extend Soviet domination to Europe, the Middle East and Asia.[9]

The Truman Doctrine

On March 12, 1947, Truman appeared before Congress to ask for $400 million in aid for Greece and its neighbor, Turkey. After arguing his case for aid to the Greek and Turkish governments, Truman discussed the implications of his policy. His reasoning was radically new.

Truman argued this was not merely a Greek civil war, but a fight against the expansion of totalitarian governments; national governments in which one person or party had absolute control over the entire nation. Truman saw Stalin's government as one such regime. He asserted that "totalitarian regimes imposed on free peoples, by direct or indirect aggression, undermine the foundations of international peace and hence the security of the United States."[10]

Truman offered a solution, a way to stop countries such as Greece from falling victim to totalitarian regimes. Since he believed "the seeds of totalitarian re-

gimes are nurtured by misery and want," the United States must be in the business of supporting "free peoples who are resisting attempted subjugation by armed minorities or by outside pressures."[11] While Truman clarified that he meant primarily financial support, the Truman Doctrine, as it came to be called, seemed to have no limits.

The president had placed something entirely new before Congress—the concept of a significant threat, a totalitarian regime that would take over the world if the United States sat idly by and allowed it. Although the speech was geared toward obtaining funding for Greece and Turkey, the Truman Doctrine itself was open-ended. This made the doctrine very influential and flexible in subsequent years, so much so that twenty-five years later, Senator William Fulbright declared, "More by far than any other factor the anti-communism of the Truman Doctrine has been the guiding spirit of American foreign policy since World War II."[12]

The Marshall Plan

The Truman Doctrine justified sending aid to free peoples anywhere, and a plan called the Marshall Plan

President Truman in 1947. Truman's policy of stopping the expansion of totalitarian regimes came to be known as the Truman Doctrine.

The Domino Theory

The domino theory did not receive its name until President Dwight D. Eisenhower labeled it as such at a White House press conference on April 7, 1954. However, while the name was new, the line of thinking was not. President Truman's administration used similar principles to guide its foreign policy, and therefore the theory was already an important part of the containment policy. The press conference can be found at PBS's Great American Speeches Website at www.pbs.org., and an excerpt from this speech in which Eisenhower explains the principles of the "domino effect" is included below.

Finally, you have broader considerations that might follow what you would call the "falling domino" principle. You have a row of dominoes set up, you knock over the first one, and what will happen to the last one is the certainty that it will go over very quickly. So you could have a beginning of a disintegration that would have the most profound influences. . . .

When we come to the possible sequence of events, the loss of Indochina, of Burma, of Thailand, of the Peninsula, and Indonesia falling, now you begin to talk about areas that not only multiply the disadvantages that you would suffer through the loss of materials, sources of materials, but now you are talking about millions and millions of people. . . .

So, the possible consequences of the loss are just incalculable to the free world.

George Marshall spoke of European recovery and made an offer to all of Europe:

It would be neither fitting nor efficacious for this Government to undertake to draw up unilaterally a program designed to place Europe on its feet economically. This is the business of the Europeans. The initiative, I think, must come from Europe.

The role of this country should consist of friendly aid in the drafting of a European program and of later support of such a program so far as it may be practical for us to do so. The program should be a joint one, agreed to by a number, if not all, European nations.[13]

In other words, interested European nations should get together, discuss the money needed, and send the United States the bill.

Representatives of both eastern and western European nations gathered in Paris less than three weeks later to take the United States up on this offer. However, the Russians soon pulled out of the meeting and took all of their satellite nations with them because, as they saw it, the Americans were trying to use their financial resources to unfairly influence other countries. Sixteen states remained, drew up a joint plan for economic recovery, and received $13 billion in U.S. aid over the next four years. Western Europe went on to experience a dramatic eco-

soon evolved from this line of thinking. The Plan came about because Europe was in economic crisis after World War II. In a June 5, 1947, commencement address at Harvard University, Secretary of State nomic recovery, which in turn significantly reduced Communist Party followings in these nations. Truman's reasoning seemed to be correct: removing poverty, misery, and want from Europe seemed to reduce the threat of totalitarian regimes.

Containment

Following Marshall's address at Harvard, an article entitled "The Sources of Soviet Conduct" appeared in the magazine *Foreign Affairs*. The article's author remained anonymous, signing his work simply "X." In reality, the author was George F. Kennan, and the article reworked and built upon his long telegram to the State Department roughly a year and a half before.

In the article, Kennan provided a clear and concise explanation of a policy that the United States would follow for the duration of the Cold War—containment. According to X, the main concern of the Soviet government was to "make sure that it has filled every nook and cranny available to it in the basin of world

Russian foreign ministers (foreground) greet Secretary of State George Marshall (center) upon his arrival in Moscow for a 1947 delegation.

power. But if it finds unassailable barriers in its path, it accepts these philosophically and accommodates itself to them."[14] In other words, the Soviets would continue their expansionist ways until they found a barrier in their path.

Therefore, it followed that the "United States policy toward the Soviet Union must be that of long-term, patient but firm and vigilant containment of Russian expansive tendencies." This could be achieved by confronting "the Russians with unalterable counter-force at every point where they show signs of encroaching upon the interests of a peaceful and stable world."[15]

This, then, was containment policy. The United States would not go around attacking Communist nations. However, wherever the Soviets tried to expand their influence, the United States would apply counterforce and thereby contain communism. Fears of appeasement, Kennan's long telegram, Winston Churchill's iron curtain speech, the Truman Doctrine, and the Marshall Plan had all been small steps in the evolution of this policy. And over the course of the Cold War, the United States would become entangled, embroiled, and entrenched in the affairs of a number of nations around the globe in its attempt to contain communism.

Chapter 2

Berlin

The Cold War began in earnest over the very country that had started both world wars—Germany—and its capital city of Berlin. It was here that the first major divisions were drawn between East and West, and more than four decades later, it was here that these divisions were erased at the Cold War's end.

A Divided City

In February 1945 the Allies (United States, Soviet Union, Great Britain, and France) met at Yalta, a city in the Ukraine, to discuss military questions. Since it was clear the end of the war in Europe was near, the Allies also made some decisions about what to do with Germany once it was defeated. The most pressing question at the time was whether or not Germany should be left in one piece and allowed to exist as a nation or be completely dismantled. While the Allies refused to make a final decision, for the time being

they decided to divide the German nation into four occupation zones (one zone to be administered by each of the Allies) and the German capital of Berlin into four corresponding zones.

When the Big Three (United States, USSR, and Great Britain) reconvened at Potsdam, Germany, in July, they established a Control Council to administer the country. The council was made up of the Commanders in Chief (C in Cs) of each of the four zones, and each C in C had a veto. Thus, decisions had to be unanimous in order to take effect.

It was easy for the Allies to agree in theory that all decisions about the administration of Germany should be unanimous, but it proved nearly impossible to reach consensus in practice. Therefore, each of the four Allies began to administer its own zone in its own way, and distinctly separate zones developed as a result. Over time, the United States, Great Britain, and France merged their

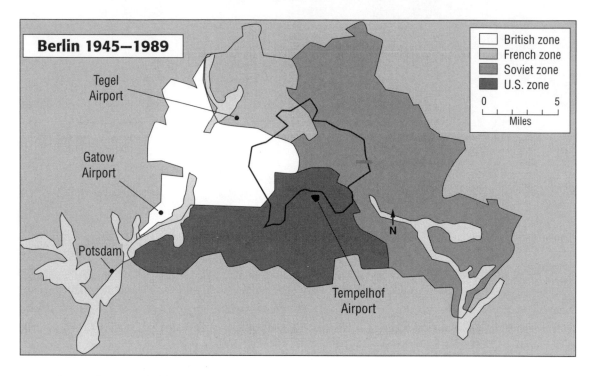

zones into what would become West Germany, and the Soviets created East Germany. Similarly, Berlin was split into West Berlin and East Berlin, and because it was in the Soviet zone of Germany, West Berlin was completely surrounded by East Germany. This east-west division remained for the rest of the Cold War. In the case of the German nation, each area was spread out over thousands of acres of land. However, in the city of Berlin, the division separated neighbors and families. Now, the grocery store down the block was technically in another country.

The German Question

A great deal of the trouble that would erupt in West Berlin in the early years of the Cold War was the direct result of differences of opinion about how to answer the "German Question." This question dominated diplomatic discussions in the immediate postwar world. The question was now that Germany was defeated and Hitler was dead, what role should Germany play in the world?

The problem with the German Question was that it had two distinctly different answers. While all four nations wanted a unified Germany, the Western powers and the Soviets did not see eye to eye on the role it should play. The United States, Great Britain, and France—the three nations that controlled West Germany—saw Germany as the key to rebuilding Western Europe and making it prosperous again. Since they needed German industry to assist in the recovery of the European economy, these Western nations worked in their sectors to create a strong, economically powerful Germany by using monies from the Marshall Plan to rebuild industry and get Germany back on track.

Two West Berlin girls stand behind a barbed wire barricade and talk to their grandparents in the Eastern zone of the city.

The Soviets wanted the exact opposite. They feared an economically powerful Germany would rearm and wage war. Therefore, they wanted to make sure Germany was weak, and the Soviets worked in their sector to achieve this goal by exacting reparations (money and goods that a defeated nation is forced to pay to the victorious nations after a war), which both accelerated Soviet economic recovery and postponed that of Germany. Thus, instead of agreeing on a solution to the German Question, the Soviets and the Western nations had simply decided to solve the problem in their own way in their own sectors.

The Berlin Blockade

During this early period, tensions mounted between the Soviets and the rest of the Allies. Stalin thought the U.S. plan to create an economically strong state of West Germany was evidence of America's aggression against Russia. To make matters worse, he was faced with a powerful West Berlin in the heart of the Soviet zone, and given the choice between living in economically strong West Berlin or weak and impoverished East Germany, people kept choosing to go west. Stalin therefore wanted to get the Western powers out of West Berlin, and he attempted

Soviet police inspect a truck during the 1948 Berlin Blockade.

to do so in what became known as the Berlin Blockade.

On April 1, 1948, the Soviets began a limited blockade and stopped U.S., British, and French trains bound for Berlin just as they entered the Soviet zone. Here the trains were delayed for many hours and eventually turned around and sent back to where they came from, which made it very inconvenient for the Western nations to get supplies into West Berlin in a timely manner. However, the Soviets did not completely block West Berlin from the Allies at this time.

Then, in June, the battle for West Berlin escalated. The United States, Great Britain, and France announced plans to create a West German state in the three united zones that they administered. They also prepared to replace the Reichsmark with a new currency to stabilize the economy in their combined zone. Called the Deutsche mark (DM), this currency was introduced in the three western zones—but not West Berlin—on June 20,

1948. Three days later, the Soviets introduced their own currency reform in their sector and announced it as the new—and only—currency for Berlin as a whole. The very same day, the Western nations introduced the DM in West Berlin, and it quickly became clear that the people of Berlin had more confidence in the Western currency. Realizing that the preference for the DM would severely undermine the East German economy, Stalin took immediate action. He decided to protect the East Germany economy by forcing the Western powers out of the city, and he hoped this would also delay West German statehood.

To this end, on June 24, 1948, the Soviets stopped all rail, road, and water traffic into West Berlin, leaving more than 2 million West Berlin citizens stranded in the midst of East Germany with very limited supplies. The blockade was completely legal, since the Big Three's agreement about Berlin at the Potsdam Conference contained no guarantees for rail, road, or water access to the city. When the United States cried foul play, arguing this agreement was implicitly understood, Soviet

The Berlin Blockade

Public support of the Berlin Airlift varied greatly as is shown by the following two excerpts from communications of the period. The first excerpt is from a letter dated September 12, 1948, written by U.S. citizen Philip Johnston to President Harry Truman expressing his opinion about the Berlin Crisis. The second excerpt is from a June 25, 1948, telegram to President Truman from Alfred A. Bingham, Chairman of the Association for a Democratic Germany. The letter and the telegram can be found in their entirety at the Truman Presidential Museum & Library website at www.trumanlibrary.org.

Johnston's Letter

The so-called "Berlin Crisis" is entirely an outgrowth of your own incredible stupidity. When you attended the Potsdam Confrence (*sic*) to arrange final details for the occupation of Germany, it was your duty to look out for American interests and insist upon the establishment of a corridor to the American zone for ingress and egress to the city. This you failed to do. . . .

You seem to be willing and even eager to force this country into a war with Russia merely for the purpose of "saving face." If you do this, the blame for such a war will rest upon your shoulders, and the blood of American boys butchered in this war will be on your head.

Bingham's Telegram

RUSSIAN EFFORTS TO DRIVE WESTERN POWERS FROM BERLIN ARE A CRUCIAL CHALLENGE TO AMERICAN FOREIGN POLICY. SURRENDER WOULD DELIVER TO RUSSIAN VENGENCE TWO MILLION GERMANS WHO HAVE DEFIED COMMUNIST TOTALITARIANISM. THERE ARE DISTURBING RUMORS TO EVACUATE BERLIN BECAUSE OF RUSSIAN BLOCKADE. . . . WE URGE YOU TO MAKE THIS COUNTRYS POSITION UNMISTAKABLE BY DECLARING THAT UNDER ALL CIRCUMSTANCES SHORT OF WAR WE WILL REMAIN IN BERLIN ambassador Alexander S. Payushkin responded that the Western powers had disregarded numerous agreements by creating West Germany and introducing currency reform. As a result, Payushkin wrote, the blockade was undertaken for the "defense of the economy for the Soviet zones against its disorganization."[16]

General Lucius Clay, the C in C of the American zone, expressed his opinion of the Soviet blockade of West Berlin as well as its immediate effect:

> When the order of the Soviet Military Administration to close all rail traffic from the western zones went into effect at 6:00 AM on the morning of June 24, 1948, the three western sectors of Berlin, with a civilian population of about 2,500,000 people, became dependent on reserve stocks and airlift replacements. It was one of the most ruthless efforts in modern times to use mass starvation for political coercion.[17]

The Berlin Airlift

The Berlin Blockade was the first real confrontation of the Cold War. One day the two nations had a tense alliance; the next they faced off over Berlin and decided whether or not to go to war. Stalin had made his choice, and now it was time for U.S. president Harry Truman to make his—whether to fight for West Berlin or leave.

In Truman's view, the USSR was trying to gain new territory and he needed to provide counterforce to make them retreat. Believing the loss of West Berlin would leave all of Europe vulnerable, Truman decided the United States needed to hold its ground and thereby contain communism. He summed up his decision succinctly to Secretary of the Navy James Forrestal: "We [are] going to stay period."[18] He later pointed out that he meant short of war.

However, getting supplies to West Berlin without going to war with the Soviets was a very tricky business. While more forceful measures involving troops and tanks were entertained, the Truman administration instead settled on supplying the people of West Berlin with food, medical supplies, and other necessities through a massive airlift. Oddly, while the Western nations had failed to ensure rail, road, or water access to West Berlin at the Potsdam Conference, written provisions were made guaranteeing three air corridors—specified routes that Western planes could take into the city. They now used these corridors to bring supplies to the West German population. Suddenly, some of the very same pilots who had bombed Berlin three years earlier were cheered as heroes for the supplies they brought to the city. Captain Earl Overholser, a U.S. soldier stationed in Berlin at the time, explained:

> One of my jobs . . . is to handle all the grateful Berlin citizens who show up.

West Berlin children cheer an American cargo plane during the Berlin Airlift.

Seems to me I've met every German in Berlin. They come down here, clutching extremely valuable heirlooms against their breasts, and want to make a little ceremony of giving the stuff to the pilots. Or some child will show up with flowers or a valued picture book. It's no act either. An old man so thin you could see through him showed up a few days ago with a watch that would have fed him for months on the black market. He insisted on giving it to an American. He called it "a little token from an old and grateful heart."[19]

Originally the airlift, called Operation Vittles, was intended to be a temporary solution—to buy the United States more time while another approach was formulated. However, in the end, it was the solution in and of itself. The airlift was an extraordinary undertaking. The U.S. Air Force and the British Royal Air Force supplied the planes and pilots while the French built a new airfield for the airlift. According to the U.S. Air Forces in Europe website, over the course of the next 324 days 278,228 flights delivered 2.3 million tons of supplies to West Berlin. In a remarkable effort on April 16, 1949, the combined U.S. and British Air Forces

German freight workers take a break after receiving a shipment of American care packages in 1949.

mounted a maximum effort known as the Easter Parade, in which 1,398 sorties (one landing in Berlin every minute) delivered 12,940 short tons of supplies in one day.

After ten and a half months, it became apparent to Stalin that the blockade would not achieve any of the objectives he had hoped it would. The Western powers remained in Berlin, and to make matters worse from Stalin's perspective, the people of West Berlin now liked their former

enemies, because the United States and Great Britain had come to their aid. In addition, the formation of the West German state was proceeding at the same pace as before. Therefore, on May 12, 1949, Stalin lifted the blockade, and the United States boasted its first success in its effort to contain communism—counterforce had been applied, and the Soviets had retreated as predicted.

However, this victory came at a price. Over the course of the blockade there were 733 incidents between Soviet and Allied aircraft, and in the more than ten months that hundreds of thousands of airlift missions had been flown, 39 British, 31 American, and 5 German airmen were killed. The two superpowers had, at times, been on the verge of war, although they never waged it. The Soviets buzzed U.S. planes but never shot one down, and the United States never sent tanks into the Soviet sector to force an entry. This was truly a Cold War, constantly teetering on the edge of military conflict between the two superpowers but never falling over that edge.

An Aching Tooth

The Western triumph was only a temporary victory, since both the Berlin Blockade and airlift had solved little. It had

28

showcased U.S. determination to hold West Berlin, and communism had been successfully contained through a show of force for the first time. However, all the underlying problems that led to the blockade remained unresolved when it was lifted. This led Soviet leader, Nikita Khrushchev, Stalin's successor, to compare the situation in Berlin to an "aching tooth." For nearly a decade, the United States and USSR put up with this toothache until Khrushchev decided to "have it out."[20]

Khrushchev made a bold move based on the Soviet's newfound atomic superiority. In 1957 the Soviet Union launched its first intercontinental ballistic missile, proving its superior missile technology. This momentary military superiority gave Khrushchev the upper hand in negotiations with the United States, and he seized it.

The first Allied road convoy enters Berlin on May 14, 1949, two days after Stalin lifted the blockade.

On November 10, 1958, he demanded that the United States, Great Britain, and France withdraw their troops from West Berlin, at which point it would become a "free city." If no agreement was reached in six months, Khrushchev threatened to turn over the access routes to the East Germans who would most assuredly deny access. The United States and its allies once again decided to stay in West Berlin, threatening to use military force to resolve the issue if necessary.

Thus, nine years after the Berlin blockade, the Soviets and the Americans were once again fighting over the same issues, and once again the city of Berlin was caught in the fray. This time the situation did not escalate to another blockade. No agreement was reached, the six-month deadline passed, and nothing happened. At this point, Khrushchev was not ready to take any active steps to remove the tooth.

The Berlin Wall

Two years later, matters had gotten worse for the East German state. West Berlin was completely accessible to East Germans, and given the choice between impoverished East Germany and the strong economy of West Berlin, a great number of East Germans were choosing the latter. In fact, roughly two hundred thousand people were leaving each year. This included a significant number of young people and skilled laborers. East Germany was losing the most productive part of its workforce to West Berlin. East German leader, Walter Ulbricht, explained the problem to Khrushchev in November 1960:

> The situation in Berlin has become complicated, not in our favor. West Berlin has strengthened economically. This is seen in the fact that about 50,000 workers from East Berlin are now still working in West Berlin. Thus, a part of the qualified working force goes to work in West Berlin, since there are higher salaries there. . . . Why don't we raise our salaries? . . . First of all, we don't have the means. Secondly, even if we raised their salary, we could not satisfy their purchasing power with the goods that we have, and they would buy things with that money in West Berlin.[21]

Khrushchev again tried to negotiate the situation. In a meeting with President John F. Kennedy in Vienna, he demanded the United States, Great Britain, and France leave West Berlin, and he reestablished another six-month deadline. Historian Arthur Schlesinger Jr. describes a subsequent exchange between the two men: "Kennedy replied that so drastic an alteration in the world balance of power was unacceptable. Khrushchev said, if America wanted war over Berlin, there was nothing the Soviet Union could do about it. . . . Kennedy commented, 'It will be a cold winter.'"[22]

Kennedy, like Truman and Eisenhower before him, believed that commu-

The Berlin Crisis

On June 3 and 4, 1961, in Vienna, Austria, Khrushchev and Kennedy discussed the situation in Berlin. Khrushchev had made it clear that the Western powers had six months to leave the city of West Berlin or their access routes would be cut off and they would be forced out. In a July 25, 1961, speech to the American people, Kennedy stated his resolve to defend West Berlin from communism. An excerpt from that speech appears below. The speech in its entirety can be found at www.cnn.com.

> The immediate threat to free men is in West Berlin. But that isolated outpost is not an isolated problem. The threat is worldwide. Our effort must be equally wide and strong and not be obsessed by any single manufactured crisis. We face a challenge in Berlin . . . We face a challenge in our own hemisphere, and indeed wherever else the freedom of human beings is at stake. . . .
>
> We cannot and will not permit the communists to drive us out of Berlin, either gradually or by force. For the fulfillment of our pledge to that city is essential to the morale and security of Western Germany, to the unity of Western Europe, and to the faith of the entire free world.

nism could not be allowed to spread to West Berlin. In a July 25, 1961, speech to the American people, he argued that the "immediate threat" was to West Berlin, but "The threat is worldwide" and added that the United States faced a challenge against the "dangers of communism" wherever "the freedom of human beings [was] at stake."[23] Kennedy decided the

United States must stand its ground and contain communism. He resolved that U.S. troops would stay put in West Berlin.

Time ticked by, and the United States built up its reserve forces in preparation for a fight. However, as was the case throughout the Cold War, that fight never occurred. Instead, Khrushchev found a different solution to the problem—on August 13, 1961, the Soviets suddenly began to build a wall that eventually surrounded West Berlin, thereby making it completely inaccessible to East Germans. This effectively stopped people from leaving East Germany and ended Soviet attempts to force the Western powers out of West Berlin. However, it also dealt a significant blow to Soviet claims that the people of East Germany desired communism. There was no denying the fact that the Berlin Wall, complete with armed guards and watchtowers, was designed to intimidate East Germans into staying in their own country. The United States protested, but in private Kennedy was said to be relieved—after all, the Wall maintained the status quo, and communism had been contained without military confrontation between the superpowers.

The Wall Comes Tumbling Down

The Wall effectively neutralized the conflict over Berlin. From the time it was built in 1961 until it came down in 1989, the Soviets and the United States never again had cause to fight over Western presence in the heart of East Germany. Over the next twenty-eight years, the Wall stopped the flood of East Germans moving to the West. During this time, roughly 5,000 East Germans succeeded in escaping over the Wall—about 179 per year. This was in stark comparison to the more than 200,000 that left each year before the Wall was constructed. Fear kept many

Russian premier Nikita Khrushchev (right) greets President Kennedy upon the president's arrival in Vienna on June 3, 1961, just months before the Berlin Wall was constructed.

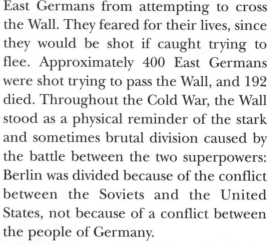

East Germans from attempting to cross the Wall. They feared for their lives, since they would be shot if caught trying to flee. Approximately 400 East Germans were shot trying to pass the Wall, and 192 died. Throughout the Cold War, the Wall stood as a physical reminder of the stark and sometimes brutal division caused by the battle between the two superpowers: Berlin was divided because of the conflict between the Soviets and the United States, not because of a conflict between the people of Germany.

Near the end of the Cold War, in April 1986, Soviet leader Mikhail Gorbachev came to believe the Soviet system was in need of reform. He launched a two-pronged program of *perestroika* (restructuring) and *glasnost* (openness). This program led Hungary, Poland, Lithuania, Estonia, and Latvia to declare their sovereignty by November 9, 1989, on which day thousands of East Germans gathered at the Berlin Wall. The people began chanting, "*Wir sind das Volk* (we are the people)" and singing the German version of "for he's a jolly good fellow." Unlike earlier protests, the East German police did not fire

Tear Down This Wall

On June 12, 1987, President Ronald Reagan stood in West Berlin in front of the Berlin Wall and called upon the Soviet premier Mikhail Gorbachev to tear it down. Gorbachev was attempting to reform the Soviet system by offering citizens more freedom, and Reagan was pushing Gorbachev to do even more. While the Wall would remain a divisive barrier for two more years, in 1989 the East German people did begin to tear it down, and the division between West and East Berlin ended. The following is an excerpt from Reagan's June 12, 1987, speech, which can be found at the Reagan Foundation's website at www.reaganfoundation.com.

Behind me stands a wall that encircles the free sectors of this city, part of a vast system of barriers that divides the entire continent of Europe. From the Baltic, south, those barriers cut across Germany in a gash of barbed wire, concrete, dog runs, and guard towers. Farther south, there may be no visible, no obvious wall. But there remain armed guards and checkpoints all the same—still a restriction on the right to travel, still an instrument to impose upon ordinary men and women the will of a totalitarian state. Yet it is here in Berlin where the wall emerges most clearly; here, cutting across [the] city, where the news photo and the television screen have imprinted this brutal division of a continent upon the mind of the world. . . .

And [in recent years] the Soviets themselves may, in a limited way, be coming to understand the importance of freedom. We hear much from Moscow about a new policy of reform and openness. Some political prisoners have been released. Certain foreign news broadcasts are no longer being jammed. Some economic enterprises have been permitted to operate with greater freedom from state control.

Are these the beginnings of profound changes in the Soviet state? Or are they token gestures, intended to raise false hopes in the West, or to strengthen the Soviet system without changing it? We welcome change and openness; for we believe that freedom and security go together, that the advance of human liberty can only strengthen the cause of world peace. There is one sign the Soviets can make that would be unmistakable, that would advance dramatically the cause of freedom and peace.

General Secretary Gorbachev, if you seek peace, if you seek prosperity for the Soviet Union and Eastern Europe, if you seek liberalization: Come here to this gate! Mr. Gorbachev, open this gate! Mr. Gorbachev, tear down this wall!

upon the crowds. Instead, the protesters chanted and sang, began to break apart sections of the Wall, and danced atop it. While the Wall remained standing—parts of it still stand today—its power to divide a nation was gone. There would be no more East German civilians shot trying to flee to the West. East Germans were now free to enter West Germany and vice versa. After more than twenty-eight years of being divided, Berlin was reunited again.

Korea: Containing Communism in Asia

In 1950 the Cold War shifted location. Previously, the tension, posturing, and exchange of rhetoric between the two superpowers had been confined to issues in Europe, and the United States had been willing to fight to contain communism in Europe where its vital interests were at stake. However, with a series of threatening events unfolding in Asia, the United States became interested in containing communism there and brought the fight against communism to a global level.

Two Victories for Communism

As the United States moved into the new year of 1949, American fears of Soviet power were soothed by two things: For one, the United States was the only nation in the world whose scientists knew how to construct nuclear weapons. Secondly, it appeared as though in China Chiang Kai-shek's Nationalist forces would defeat the Communist forces led by Mao Tse-tung.

However, on August 29, 1949, the first of these reassuring conditions came to an end when the Soviets exploded their first successful atomic bomb. The atomic monopoly the United States had enjoyed for five years was gone and, with it, the sense of security that monopoly provided. Roughly one month later, the Chinese Communist forces defeated the Nationalist forces, and Mao declared the Communist People's Republic of China.

Shaken by the Soviet's newfound atomic capability along with what critics called the "loss of China," President Truman asked the State and Defense Departments to prepare an analysis of Soviet and American military capabilities. The result was National Security Council Paper no. 68 (NSC-68). The paper was a testament to the heightened sense of fear and paranoia about the Soviet Union that was sweeping the nation. Its authors argued that the USSR was bent on taking over the world and forcefully made a case to step up containment efforts. The delicate balance of power between communism and anticommunism was not to be disturbed. NSC-68 claimed "the assault on free institutions is world-wide now, and in the context of the present polarization of power a defeat of free institutions anywhere is a

A military brigade led by Mao Tse-tung (center) enters the city of Peiping, China, in 1949. The "loss of China" to communism had significant implications for the Cold War.

defeat everywhere."[24] It recommended the United States build up its military strength, too, if it wanted to successfully contain communism around the world.

NSC-68 greatly enlarged the containment policy. Originally, the United States thought it was necessary to contain communism only in areas around the globe where its interests were threatened. Now NSC-68 argued that the loss of the most seemingly insignificant country could set off a chain reaction that would end in Soviet world domination. It was therefore necessary to combat communism anywhere and everywhere around the world. NSC-68 was given to Truman on April 7, 1950. Roughly three months later he made a decision that clearly attested to his belief in its reasoning when he chose to contain communism in an area where there were relatively few American interests at stake—Korea.

North and South Korea

At the end of World War II, the United States and the Soviet Union agreed to divide Korea at the thirty-eighth parallel, a longitudinal line that split the country roughly in half, with the Soviets occupying the north and the Americans the south. A Communist government under the leadership of Kim Il Sung

NSC-68

In response to Soviet development of atomic weapons and the "loss" of China, President Truman asked the State and Defense Departments to prepare an analysis of Soviet and American capabilities in war and in peace. The result was NSC-68, and in this excerpt its authors argue that containment rests on the shoulders of "superior overall power." This line of thinking, that the United States must stay ahead in the arms race in order to contain communism, became an essential part of the arms race and the Cold War. NSC-68 can be found in its entirety at Federation of American Scientists website, www.fas.org.

> As for the policy of "containment," it is one which seeks by all means short of war to (1) block further expansion of Soviet power, (2) expose the falsities of Soviet pretensions, (3) induce a retraction of the Kremlin's control and influence, and (4) in

general, so foster the seeds of destruction within the Soviet system that the Kremlin is brought at least to the point of modifying its behavior to conform to generally accepted international standards.

It was and continues to be cardinal in this policy that we possess superior overall power in ourselves or in dependable combination with other likeminded nations. One of the most important ingredients of power is military strength. In the concept of "containment," the maintenance of a strong military posture is deemed to be essential for two reasons: (1) as an ultimate guarantee of our national security and (2) as an indispensable backdrop to the conduct of the policy of "containment." Without superior aggregate military strength, . . . a policy of "containment" . . . is no more than a policy of bluff.

was established in the north, while in the south Syngman Rhee headed up an authoritarian, anti-Communist regime. Kim Il Sung formed the Democratic People's Republic of Korea in the north, and Rhee created the Republic of Korea (ROK) in the south. However, neither Kim nor Rhee was satisfied; both men wanted to rule over a united Korea, and a civil war broke out between the two sides.

The result, as historian Walter LaFeber points out, was that "Both superpowers found themselves trapped in a bloody civil conflict, Korean killing Korean, which . . . claimed 100,000 lives after 1946 and *before* the formal beginning in June 1950 of what Americans call the 'Korean

War.'"[25] The matter was put before the United Nations, which set up a Commission on Korea (UNCOK) to work for reunification.

In many ways, Korea had become a pawn in the game of the Cold War. While the Korean people may have wanted reunification, a united Korea was not in the best interest of either superpower. Reunification meant that the whole of Korea would become either Communist or non-Communist. If it became Communist, the United States would lose an anti-Communist ally, just as the Soviets would lose a Communist ally should a non-Communist government come to power. Rather than risk losing their footholds in

Asia, both the United States and the USSR preferred that Korea remain peacefully divided. This showed in the United Nations, where the United States and the USSR squared off on Korea.

The UN passed a motion declaring the ROK the only legitimate government for all of Korea. The Soviet counterproposal to recognize Kim Il Sung's regime as the only legitimate government was soundly defeated. While in reality the issue remained completely unresolved, the United States formally recognized the ROK, and soon after, Soviet and American troops left the country, leaving the Korean people to their own devices. However, the Soviets left behind a well-prepared North Korean army, whereas the United States had done little to fortify Rhee's army in the south.

Take two authoritarian leaders who want to rule over Korea in its entirety, give one diplomatic recognition as the rightful leader, give the other one better military forces, and the result is a recipe for war. Without the superpowers there to stop it, the civil conflict in Korea worsened, and it was only a matter of time until the conflict escalated into all-out war.

The Prelude to War

On June 25, 1950, North Korean forces flooded across the thirty-eighth parallel and quickly made their way southward to what they thought would be instant

South Korean president Syngman Rhee proudly displays the Korean flag in 1950.

victory. After years of border skirmishes and smaller attacks, this still came as a surprise to the ROK and most of the rest of the world. It was not, however, a surprise to Stalin, who had given Kim Il Sung the go-ahead and support. As P.M.H. Bell points out, the go-ahead was given on certain conditions: "the North must be sure of quick success; there must be no likelihood of American intervention; and no escalation into war."[26]

The Soviets assisted Kim Il Sung in planning the attack and supplied him with military equipment, believing victory could be achieved under these conditions. Rhee's forces were weak and could easily be defeated; and the Soviets did not think the United States would intervene, primarily because the U.S. government had said as much. Time and again U.S. officials implied that American interests were not at stake in South Korea, that it was outside of the U.S. defense perimeter and would have to fend for itself should it come under attack.

The United States Enters

However, Soviet hopes that the United States would not come to South Korea's aid were soon dashed. Truman's initial response to the invasion was to order U.S. general Douglas MacArthur to send supplies to the South Koreans from his outpost in Tokyo. The United States then convened an emergency session of the United Nations Security Council and passed a resolution labeling the North Koreans as the aggressors and calling for an immediate cease-fire and the removal of North Korean troops from the south.

The resolution achieved little beyond placing blame, and two days later the fighting had worsened. On June 27 Truman ordered United States Air Force and Navy troops into action. That same day, the Security Council passed a resolution asking members of the UN to "furnish assistance to the Republic of Korea as may be necessary to repel the armed attack and to restore international peace and security in the area."[27] June 29 and 30 marked the official commitment of U.S. ground troops to defend South Korea.

Why Korea?

Thus, in a matter of days, President Truman committed U.S. troops to a war in Korea, a country defined as outside of the U.S. defense perimeter just months before. South Korea's increased importance in the eyes of the American government was the result of a number of factors. The loss of China, the Soviet atomic bomb, and the predictions and recommendations of NSC-68 all played a significant role in the decision because they increased U.S. fears of a great Soviet plan for world domination. In this plan, some U.S. officials saw Korea as the first domino, which, once it was knocked over, would allow the Soviets and the Chinese Communists to take over all of Asia and, eventually, Europe.

Secretary of State Dean Acheson saw the invasion in this light. In 1950 he told

The UN Security Council's Resolution

On June 25, 1950, the United Nations Security Council passed a resolution calling for North Korea to withdraw its forces to the thirty-eighth parallel and hostilities to cease. The resolution passed 9-0 with Yugoslavia abstaining. Had the Soviet ambassador been present, the resolution would certainly have been vetoed. However, he was absent because the Soviets were boycotting the Security Council for its failure to recognize Communist China. The following is an excerpt from the June 25 Resolution. It can be found in its entirety at www.trumanlibrary.org.

> [The Security Council] Noting with grave concern the armed attack upon the Republic of Korea by forces from North Korea,
>
> Determine that this action constitutes a breach of peace,
>
> Calls for the immediate cessation of hostilities; and

Calls upon the authorities of North Korea to withdraw forthwith their armed forces to the thirty-eighth parallel.

Requests the United Nations Commission on Korea to communicate its fully considered recommendations on the situation with the least possible delay.

to observe the withdrawal of the North Korean forces to the thirty-eighth parallel.

to keep the Security Council informed on the execution of this resolution.

Calls upon all members to render every assistance to the United Nations in the execution of this resolution and to refrain from giving assistance to the North Korean authorities.

The UN Security Council votes on a resolution calling for North Korea to withdraw its troops from South Korea in 1950.

advisors, "The invasion of Southern Korea cannot be regarded as an isolated incident. . . . [It] is a clear indication of the pattern of aggression under a general international Communist plan." Acheson urged "quick affirmative action" in such instances to forestall "a deterioration of the entire Far Eastern situation."[28] Truman agreed. He argued if the United States did not contain communism in Korea, the Soviets would sponsor invasions such as these around the world until it was necessary to go to war to stop them. Truman (falsely) saw the North Korean assault as a Soviet-led venture and an attempt to test American determination and resolve to fight communism. He decided to send troops, a decision that would prove to be a costly one, resulting in a three-year war and the death of over fifty thousand U.S. soldiers.

From Containing to "Rolling Back" Communism

Thus, the United States became involved in a war to contain communism by defending South Korea from its North Korean Communist attackers. The United States did so as part of a United Nations effort in which the American armed forces and the ROK forces made up the majority of troops and were supported by units from fourteen other nations, most notably Great Britain and Turkey. U.S. general Douglas MacArthur was named the commander in chief of the UN forces, and the goal at the outset was to drive back the North Korean invasion and reestablish South Korea's border at the thirty-eighth parallel.

In the early stages of the war, it did not look as though the UN forces would accomplish this goal. The Communist forces drove them back into the southeastern corner of Korea near Pusan, and the defensive line established by the U.S. and South Korean forces to protect this small area looked extremely vulnerable, as though the North Koreans could defeat them at any moment. It appeared Kim Il Sung would get the quick victory he had hoped for.

However, General MacArthur and his forces stood in the way of that victory, and on September 15, 1950, MacArthur made an unexpected landing behind enemy lines at Inchon. This caused a great deal of confusion for the North Korean forces and, fearing encirclement, they retreated. This allowed the UN forces to recapture Seoul, the capital of South Korea. They had successfully driven Kim Il Sung's forces out of South Korea. The initial goal of the UN forces was accomplished. Communism had been successfully contained.

Now the question became whether or not to "roll back" communism. Containment policy clearly stated that the United States would not attack any existing Communist nations; its goal was only to stop any more nations from "falling" to communism. However, with North Korean forces retreating, the United Nations had the opportunity to pursue them, unify

American troops land at Inchon on September 15, 1950.

Korea under Rhee's government, and thereby deal communism a loss: the opportunity to "roll it back."

On September 27 Truman gave MacArthur the go-ahead to proceed north of the thirty-eighth parallel as long as no Chinese or Russian resistance was encountered. As historian Walter LaFeber points out, "Given MacArthur's self-confidence, if not arrogance, that was an invitation for him to drive to the Yalu [the river that divides North Korea from China]."[29]

The Chinese Contain the United States

As MacArthur advanced into North Korea, the United States waited tensely to see whether China would intervene on behalf of their fellow Communists. The U.S. Central Intelligence Agency (CIA) was asked to prepare an intelligence report

on the matter. Author Nathan Miller describes the CIA's conclusions:

North Korean soldiers surrender to American Marines at Inchon.

Regarding China as little more than a Soviet satellite, CIA analysts took the position that the Chinese would intervene only if it suited the Russians. 'While full-scale Chinese Communist intervention must be regarded as a continuing possibility, consideration of all known factors leads to the conclusion that barring a Soviet decision for global war, such action is not probable in 1950,' the agency reported.[30]

Ultimately, the U.S. decision to cross the thirty-eighth parallel was incredibly costly. Roughly 80 percent of the total casualties sustained by the UN forces over the course of the war occurred as a result. At first, MacArthur was able to push northward with relative ease. However, in early October, Kim Il Sung appealed to Stalin for help. Stalin was not willing to directly commit Soviet forces and thus link his country to the war; instead, he asked Mao to send Chinese troops disguised as "volunteers."

Mao did so, and as UN troops approached the Yalu River, it became increasingly clear that the Chinese "volunteers" would not stand idly by. However, the warning signs were ignored or, in some cases, came too late, and MacArthur launched a general offensive on November 24 only to be met by Chinese troops that outnumbered his own forces. The Chinese "volunteers" were able to force the UN troops to retreat to the south of the thirty-eighth parallel. Supported by the Chinese, the North Koreans once again recaptured Seoul.

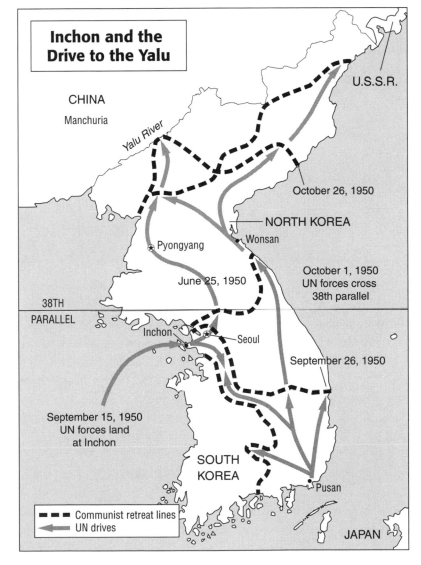

Inchon and the Drive to the Yalu

CHINA

Manchuria

Yalu River

U.S.S.R.

October 26, 1950

NORTH KOREA

Wonsan

Pyongyang

June 25, 1950

October 1, 1950
UN forces cross
38th parallel

38TH PARALLEL

Inchon

Seoul

September 26, 1950

September 15, 1950
UN forces land
at Inchon

SOUTH KOREA

Pusan

- - - Communist retreat lines
→ UN drives

JAPAN

A Limited War

In January 1951 the UN forces were finally able to stabilize the front a little more than fifty miles south of the thirty-eighth parallel. Thousands of lives had been lost only for the UN forces to end up in a worse position than when they had started their push northward. To make matters worse, the Chinese and North Korean combined forces were proving to be difficult to defeat.

At this point, disagreements between MacArthur and Truman arose over the purpose of the war. MacArthur believed that wars were

A supply warehouse is bombed during a UN advance on the North Korean port of Wonsan.

for winning and therefore advocated the expansion of the war to allow his forces to attack China in order to conquer Korea. Truman, on the other hand, saw the Korean War as a limited war with very specific goals. If he were to commit the majority of U.S. forces to defeating China, other places around the globe would be left vulnerable to Soviet attack.

This was an important piece of the policy of containment—that it was a worldwide struggle with battles fought here and there. Thus, for Truman, Korea was one battle in a much larger global war. Since the initial goal had been to push the North Korean forces back to the thirty-eighth parallel, he settled for meeting this objective now. When MacArthur continued to publicly criticize his decision, Truman dismissed him and replaced him with General Matthew B. Ridgeway.

Armistice

In 1951 General Ridgeway launched a new offensive to recapture Seoul and push the North Koreans back just to the north of the thirty-eighth parallel. The

UN forces accomplished this in July 1951, and here the line would stay, with soldiers perishing daily, for the two years it took to come to an armistice agreement. The sticking point was not a matter of military or geographical import—both sides wanted the war to end and the division between north and south to be at the thirty-eighth parallel. The sticking point was a question of what to do with prisoners of war (POWs) who did not want to return to their home countries. A number of Chinese and North Korean POWs did not want to return to their homelands. If they were not forced to return, such a mass defection would deal a significant blow to the prestige of the Communist regimes in China and North Korea. With these countries unwilling to risk such an outcome and the United States opposed to forcing the POWs to return to their homelands, armistice was impossible, and the war continued.

It took a new American president to finally break the stalemate. In 1952 Dwight D. Eisenhower became president of the United States. Since Eisenhower was a well-respected military leader during World War II, it gave him a bit more power at the bargaining table. In 1953 Eisenhower was

Truman Dismisses MacArthur

In the midst of the Korean War it became necessary for President Truman to dismiss General Douglas MacArthur from his post. MacArthur had publicly disagreed with Truman on the handling of the war in Korea. He also blamed the UN forces' November 1950 loss to the Chinese Communist army on Truman's decisions. Soon after, Truman decided to dismiss the general. Truman's April 11, 1951, statement on the matter appears below. It can be found at www.cnn.com.

With deep regret I have concluded that General of the Army Douglas MacArthur is unable to give his wholehearted support to the policies of the United States Government and of the United Nations in matters pertaining to his official duties. In view of the specific responsibilities imposed upon me by the Constitution of the United States and the added responsibility which has been entrusted to [me] by the United Nations, I have decided that I must make a change of command in the Far East. I have, therefore, relieved General MacArthur of his commands and have designated Lt. Gen. Matthew B. Ridgeway as his successor.

Full and vigorous debate on matters of national policy is a vital element in the constitutional system of our free democracy. It is fundamental, however, that military commanders must be governed by the policies and directives issued to them in the manner provided by our laws and Constitution. In time of crisis, this consideration is particularly compelling.

General MacArthur's place in history as one of our greatest commanders is fully established. The Nation owes him a debt of gratitude for the distinguished and exceptional service which he has rendered his country in posts of great responsibility. For that reason I repeat my regret at the necessity for the action I feel compelled to take in his case.

General Mark W. Clark signs the armistice ending the three-year conflict in Korea, which cost over 86,000 lives.

fed up with the deadlock and threatened to use atomic weapons against China if a settlement was not reached. Shortly thereafter, Stalin died, and whether it was his death, the threat of nuclear war, or both, the Chinese and the North Koreans agreed to allow a committee of neutral nations to work on repatriation. As a result, an armistice was concluded on July 27, 1953.

The Korean War was over. The U.S. effort to contain communism had achieved its original goal, but at a high price. Along with roughly 50,000 South Koreans and 3,000 soldiers from other

UN nations, 33,399 American soldiers died in the war. In addition, the war and the events preceding it had transformed the containment policy. The U.S. fight to stop the spread of communism was now a worldwide battle to be fought in places around the globe. Complete victory was not necessary; instead, battles were fought simply to contain the enemy.

Chapter 4

Egypt: Arab Nationalism Versus Containment

O nce the Korean armistice was complete, the U.S. focus shifted from the war in Southeast Asia to containing communism in the Middle East. The biggest Cold War prize in the region was Egypt. Its geographic location made it highly desirable, since it linked the eastern and western parts of the Arab world. In addition, Egypt boasted the largest population of all the Arab states, which meant it could potentially muster the largest military force. Its substantial population also made for a significantly large middle class that allowed Egypt to dominate the region culturally. All these factors led author Adeed Dawisha to conclude, "Egypt has been, and continues to be, the most important Arab country."[31]

While the U.S. government became entangled in the affairs of West Berlin and Korea in response to Communist aggression, its involvement in Egyptian affairs was different. It was not an attempt to halt any immediate threat, but a desire to take precautionary measures to stop Soviet expansion before it started. The Americans hoped to win the favor of Egyptian leader Gamal Abdel Nasser and then use his influence in the Middle East to convince all the Arab nations to join in the fight to contain communism.

Therefore, the United States spent a great deal of time and energy in the mid-1950s attempting to woo, cajole, and coerce Nasser's Egypt into joining America's side in the Cold War. However, this American diplomatic mission was doomed to fail, since siding with the Americans in the Cold War would have required Nasser to act in opposition to his ideology of Arab nationalism, which called for an end to Western influence and the unity of Arab peoples. When irreconcilable goals eventually forced Nasser to look to the Soviets for assistance, the United States felt threatened by this alliance, as though they had lost an important battle in the fight against communism.

A New President and a New Look

It was President Eisenhower who first focused in on Egypt as an important player in the Middle East. Eisenhower took office in 1952, and his views on the Soviet Union did not differ greatly from those of Truman. His administration also believed the Soviets were bent on world domination, but Eisenhower's Cold War approach diverged from that of his predecessor on one important issue—cost. Whereas Truman was willing to commit U.S. troops wherever they were needed to contain communism, Eisenhower realized that maintaining such a large conventional army was costing the United States a great deal of money. Truman spent $50 billion annually on defense, and Eisenhower feared this would eventually ruin the economy. Therefore, Eisenhower devised a new way to continue the worldwide containment of communism on a smaller budget; his approach came to be known as the new look.

There were two key components of the new look. The first was that nuclear weapons were cheaper than armies, so the president resolved to make more nuclear weapons and decrease the size of

Egyptian leader Gamal Abdel Nasser (center) shakes hands with Soviet premier Nikita Khrushchev in 1960.

U.S. conventional forces. In so doing, he decreased troops and doubled the nation's nuclear stockpile by 1955. Eisenhower was not afraid to threaten to use these weapons either, and he became the first U.S. president to consider atomic and nuclear bombs as conventional weapons, believing they were to "be used exactly as you would use a bullet or anything else."[32]

The other facet of Eisenhower's new look was to spread out the costs of the Cold War by persuading other nations to bear some of the financial burden. He sought to create a number of regional alliances to both contain the Soviets and minimize the U.S. costs in the event of an attack. By the time he came to power, the North Atlantic Treaty Organization (NATO) already existed as a regional alliance protecting Europe: Should one country that was a member of NATO come under attack, all the other nations would help defend it. Eisenhower soon created a Southeast Asian alliance on this model (SEATO). With these regional alliances hemming in the Soviets from the west, east, and southeast, the administration turned its eyes toward the Middle East. As a regional leader, Egypt became very important to the U.S. plan to contain communism.

The Rise of Arab Nationalism

The United States was not the first Western nation to recognize the importance of Egypt. While Egypt was never officially a British colony, the British had played a role in Egypt for more than a century. This began in the mid-1800s when the Egyptian monarchy went into debt building the Suez Canal and was forced to sell its shares in

Construction of the Suez Canal (pictured) left the Egyptian monarchy in debt, forcing the regime to sell its shares of the canal to Great Britain.

A fleet of ships approaches the newly opened Suez Canal in 1869.

the canal to Great Britain. Once they had a foothold in Egypt, the British consolidated their control. Eventually, they named it a British protectorate during World War I, completely took over the Egyptian government, and made the Egyptian populace provide them with a variety of resources they needed to fight the war.

In 1922 the British and the Egyptians concluded a treaty that declared Egypt a sovereign nation. However, the British still retained control of the Suez Canal and the right to intervene in Egyptian affairs. This was unacceptable in the eyes of many Egyptians, and, as a result, many cit-

izens disliked Western nations, in general, and Great Britain, in particular.

By the end of World War II, Egypt was in flux. The head of the Egyptian monarchy, King Farouk, was slowly losing his grip on the country. His power was waning because of the rise of a group of junior army officers who called themselves the Free Officers and espoused the ideals of Arab nationalism, which called for independence from Western interference and the union of Arab peoples based on their common history and language. Anti-British sentiments also were an important component of Arab nationalism, as was anti-Zionism. (The Zionists were members of an international movement to establish a Jewish homeland in Palestine. With assistance from the British, the Zionists were able to achieve their goal of a Jewish homeland, eventually declaring the state of Israel in May 1948.)

Many Arab nationalists saw the Zionists' control of Palestine (Israel) as illegal. To them, the Western powers were meddling in Arab affairs and giving away Arab lands to non-Arabs. Arabs of many nations were in solidarity with the plight of the Palestinians and united in an attack on Israel led by Egypt, which occurred the day after Israel declared itself a state. The Arab-Israeli war was a disaster for the Arabs, and their defeat only intensified anti-Zionism, which now became an even more important facet of Arab nationalism.

Nasser Comes to Power

This defeat also put a strain on the domestic politics of Egypt. Tension arose between the head of the Egyptian monarchy, King Farouk, and the government led by the Arab nationalist party. Violent uprisings began to occur, and in 1952 a revolution led by the nationalist Free Officers deposed the king and declared an authoritarian republic headed by General Muhammad Naguib.

Naguib became president of the new Egyptian government, but there were other Free Officers who rivaled him for this position, most notably a young colonel named Gamal Abdel Nasser. Increasing difficulties led to the extension of martial law and Naguib's resignation in February 1954. The following November, Nasser took full power of Egypt and would eventually become the most influential proponent of Arab nationalism in the world.

The United States Maneuvers to Make a Deal

Since Nasser and the Free Officers wielded a great deal of power over not just Egypt but also other Arab nations of the Middle East, the U.S. government sought to utilize their influence to contain communism in the region. Over the course of the next few years, U.S. officials would work to help the Free Officers achieve some of their goals in exchange for their allegiance in the fight against communism.

One of the Free Officers' primary goals was to end British occupation of Egypt, particularly at the Suez Canal base. As for the British, for nearly a century the Suez base had served as a stronghold for their empire in the Middle East. However, in the aftermath of World War II, Great Britain was experiencing financial difficulties, and the price of maintaining the Suez base was draining British funds. In addition, the Egyptians were clearly not happy with British occupation of the base. For these reasons, the British sought to

Fears of Nasser

In a 1996 article about Nasser's rise to power, author Donald Neff discusses the fears that Israel, Great Britain, and France had about Nasser. Neff's article can be found at www.washington-report.org.

> On July 23, 1952 . . . corrupt King Farouk of Egypt, an Albanian on his paternal side, was overthrown by a group of young military men calling themselves the Free Officers. The next day, one of the officers, Anwar Sadat, informed the nation by radio that for the first time in two thousand years Egypt was under the rule of Egyptians. Sadat spoke in the name of General Mohammed Neguib, the revolution's [so-called leader]. In fact, the real leader was Gamal Abdel Nasser. He was 34 at the time and would rule Egypt for the next 18 turbulent years. Because of his youth, Nasser hid his power behind the older Neguib for the first two years of the new regime. It was not until 1954 that he officially became prime minister and not until June 23, 1956, that he assumed the presidency.
>
> The coming to power in Egypt of the energetic young warrior sent shockwaves through Britain, France and Israel. Leaders in all three countries feared him as a galvanizing ruler who had the potential to unify the shattered Arab world at the expense of the West and Israel. As Israel's David Ben-Gurion put it: "I always feared that a personality might rise such as arose among the Arab rulers in the seventh century or like [Kemal Ataturk] who rose in Turkey after its defeat in the First World War. He raised their spirits, changed their character, and turned them into a fighting nation. There was and still is a danger that Nasser is this man."

maintain some influence in the Middle East that was not as expensive and did not antagonize Middle Eastern citizens. Thus, both sides were ready to bargain, and to gain the favor of the Free Officers, the United States was willing to mediate.

However, while coming to an agreement was beneficial to both sides, the British and the Free Officers differed as to what the terms of the agreement should be. The Free Officers wanted immediate, complete withdrawal of British troops from the base; the British wanted seven thousand uniformed troops to remain to administer the base for an indefinite period of time and the base to be fully and immediately available to the British in the event of an emergency. Somewhere between these two viewpoints, the U.S. ambassadors had to find a compromise.

Eventually, the United States was able to work with both nations to broker a deal. This was difficult since the United States wanted to please the Egyptians to gain their trust and subsequently utilize their influence to contain communism. However, on the other side of the negotiating coin lay Great Britain, whom the United States considered its most essential ally in the fight against communism.

On July 27, 1954, however, the two countries finally reached an agreement over the canal that came to be called the

Anglo-Egyptian Treaty. The British agreed to withdraw all of their combat troops over a twenty-month period and leave behind one thousand civilian technicians to maintain the base for the next seven years. The Egyptians agreed to allow the British to reactivate the base in the event of certain types of attack. When all was said and done, the United States had helped the Free Officers achieve their goal of ending British occupation, and U.S. officials believed they were one step closer to convincing them to help contain communism.

Differences of Opinion

However, after the Free Officers signed the Anglo-Egyptian agreement, they did not prove to be as thankful as the Eisen-

hower administration had hoped. In fact, once the British presence in Egypt was gone, the Free Officers began to pursue their own goals of Arab nationalism. Being proponents of Arab Nationalism, however, led the Free Officers to argue against exactly what the United States was trying to accomplish; Nasser did not want Arab nations entering into alliances with Western nations.

Over the next few years, the U.S. government refused to recognize the incompatibility of their goals with those of the Arab nationalism of the Free Officers. To

British Minister of State Anthony Nutting (left) and Gamal Abdel Nasser (right) sign the 1954 Anglo-Egyptian Treaty.

make matters more complicated, while U.S. officials still believed they could persuade Egyptian leaders to behave the way they wanted them to, they also made other arrangements in case they failed to do so. The Americans worked behind the scenes to form an alliance of Turkey, Iraq, Iran, and Pakistan (eventually called the Baghdad Pact). Since Iraq was one of Egypt's chief rivals, this only further antagonized the Egyptians.

The Alpha Plan

Once the British and the Egyptians concluded the Anglo-Egyptian Treaty, the United States quickly identified what it believed to be the next stumbling block in the road to the creation of a defense network in the Middle East—the tension between the Arab nations and Israel. The State Department argued that these tensions could erupt at any given point and move key players in the Middle East into Soviet hands. Therefore, the United States set about brokering peace between the Arabs and Israel, realizing the most influential Arab state, Egypt, would have to be in its corner in order for the peace to be successful.

The U.S. blueprint for peace came to be called the Alpha Plan. It called for an end to hostilities between Israel and Egypt. Israel would allow seventy-five thousand Palestinian refugees to return to their homes in what was now Israel, while the remaining refugees would be compensated through an international effort.

Israel would also make territorial concessions; in particular, it would relinquish its hold on the Negev desert. In exchange for Israel's concessions, the Western powers would guarantee its borders. In exchange for Egypt's cooperation, the Free Officers would receive financial and military aid from the United States.

This was a solution the United States thought would work, and, without telling either the Israelis or the Egyptians about the goals of the Alpha Plan, American officials set out to move the two countries towards such an agreement. Unfortunately for the United States, the Alpha Plan was doomed to fail because it was based more on the American desire for peace in order to build a containment network than it was on concessions that either side was actually willing to make. The Israelis were not willing to concede territory, and to enter into a peace agreement with Israel went against the Arab nationalism upon which Nasser's power and popular appeal was based. Still, the United States forged ahead to try to achieve its goal.

The Gaza Raid and the Czech Arms Purchase

On February 28, 1955, Israel significantly undermined the possibility of peace with Egypt by launching an attack on an Egyptian base in Gaza (a seaport adjacent to southwest Israel) to retaliate for Egypt's hanging of two Israeli spies. Twenty-nine Egyptian soldiers were killed in the raid, and in the process so too was any Egyp-

Israeli soldiers stop a group of Egyptian Arabs during the 1955 Gaza raid.

tian desire for peace with Israel. Nasser moved quickly to secure his nation from further aggression. He did this by calling on Arab nations to create a defensive alliance based not on communism or anticommunism, but on Arab nationalism. In March, Nasser announced the formation of an Arab alliance between Egypt, Syria, and Saudi Arabia.

After creating the Arab alliance, Nasser set about the next step in securing his nation—procuring weapons. This step would prove to be particularly offensive to the United States, which could not give military aid to Egypt because of its al-

liances with Israel and Great Britain. The Soviets stepped in and seized the opportunity to undermine the United States in the Middle East and block its efforts to contain communism in the region.

The Soviets offered the Egyptians one hundred MiG jet fighters, two hundred tanks, and some Ilyushin jet bombers in exchange for Egyptian cotton. They also hinted at the fact that they might be willing to help finance the Aswan Dam, a costly project for which Egypt had been unable to secure full funding. Nasser graciously accepted the offer for military supplies, and the USSR used the Soviet satellite nation of Czechoslovakia as a front for the deal to make it appear as though the Egyptians were purchasing arms from the Czechs instead of the Soviets.

In this way, Nasser was able to secure and arm his nation without playing by the rules of the West and making peace with Israel. Instead of signing the U.S. Alpha Plan in order to receive arms, he had created his own defense network and procured arms from the Soviets. However, the U.S. government saw this as a dangerous move toward communism and began to wonder whether Nasser himself would one day have to be "contained."

Leaders from Saudi Arabia, Syria, and Jordan pose with Nasser (third from left) in Cairo in 1957.

The Aswan Dam

After the Czech arms deal, U.S. paranoia about Soviet designs for expansion into the Middle East began to creep into U.S. foreign policy. Realizing that more leverage was necessary to gain the cooperation of Nasser, the United States found a new bargaining chip: officials began to discuss financing the building of the Egyptian Aswan Dam. Egyptian leaders had long desired a dam to harness the power of the Nile and allow Egyptian farmers to compete with farmers around the world. However, the price tag on the project was so enormous that they had not yet been able to build it. The "string" the United States attached to the financing for the dam would be that Egypt would have to enter into a peaceful agreement with Israel, thereby furthering U.S. goals in the Middle East.

However, the United States had miscalculated. The Egyptians were angry with the Israelis for attacking Egypt in the Gaza raid. If Nasser were to make peace with Israel, he would lose a significant number of the Arab nationalist supporters upon which his political power depended. The money was an enticing offer, but Nasser had refused to make peace with Israel to obtain arms from the United States to protect his nation. It was therefore unlikely that he would now make peace for money.

The Failure of the Alpha Plan Leads to Operation Omega

By March 1956 the United States had no choice but to admit the complete failure of the Alpha Plan. After years of diplomacy to try to make peace between Israel and Egypt on U.S. terms a reality, summit after summit had yielded no results. U.S. officials assumed Israel would concede territory, and it refused to do so. The American government also failed to understand that peace with Israel was antagonistic to Arab nationalism. Unable to recognize the problems with their basic assumptions, U.S. officials blamed Nasser for the failure of the Alpha Plan.

The Americans switched tactics. Since it could not get the most influential country in the Middle East on its side by wooing it, the United States would have to either coerce Nasser into helping them or make another Arab state more powerful than Egypt. In an attempt to do so, U.S. officials devised Operation Omega, a plan that sought to coerce the Free Officers to act in ways that were beneficial to the United States government while minimizing Egypt's influence in Arab affairs. Operation Omega was a two-pronged approach. The United States would work to undermine Nasser's regional power as it decreased monies to Egypt in phases. Thus, the Americans began to delay funds they had promised Nasser.

The Suez Crisis Begins

When delaying funds did not work, the United States began canceling funds altogether. When even the cancellation of some funds was not an effective way of coercing Egypt into supporting American goals, Secretary of State Dulles announced on July 19, 1956, that the Americans would cancel the $1.3 billion earmarked for the Aswan Dam project, hoping to deal Nasser a heavy political and financial blow.

Yet, just as Alpha had failed, so too would Omega, because while the West was waiting for Egypt to come crawling back, Nasser had his own ideas. He shocked the world on July 26, 1956, when he announced that Egypt would seize the Suez Canal from the British-controlled Universal Suez Canal Company. (He offered to pay shareholders a set price, so this was completely legal. However, shareholders were still being forced to sell.) Nasser promised to keep the canal open to all current users and stated he was planning

to use the company's yearly profits of $25 million to help build the dam.

Nasser waves to a crowd of supporters as he arrives in Cairo in 1956.

The International Reaction

Great Britain and France saw Nasser's seizure of the canal company as a significant threat to their oil supplies. In 1955, 67 million tons of oil had passed through the canal on its way to Europe. In addition, there was a real sense that Nasser had gotten out of hand.

Fears that Nasser would stop allowing canal use, combined with anger at Nasser for being too uppity, led the two European nations to plot a military operation to recapture the canal. Great Britain and France enlisted the aid of Israel and se-

cretly planned an attack on Egypt. The plan was simple. Israel would attack Egypt, making it appear as though France and Great Britain were not in any way linked to this decision. Then, the British and French would intervene to stop the conflict by occupying the Suez Canal to separate the Israeli and Egyptian armed forces. The three conspiring nations set their plan in motion on October 29, 1956, when Israel launched its attack.

Militarily, the maneuver was a success. However, the British had misjudged

U.S. reaction. Instead of supporting the European seizure of the canal or even simply tolerating it, in an odd move the United States acted quickly against the British and French to stop their retaking of the canal. The United States denied having any ties to the Anglo-French military expedition. It then threatened to halt funds to the UK that were to be used to support the faltering economy and cut off the Latin America oil supplies that the European nations needed to proceed with their venture. The United States then took its case to the United Nations and on November 3, 1956, the United States and USSR worked together to force the British and French to accept a cease-fire and evacuate the canal area.

The reasoning of U.S. officials that led to what historians Felix Gilbert and David Clay Large have called a "zig-zag course of American policy,"[33] has baffled historians just as it did Great Britain and France at the time. Scholar Ray Takeyh offers some possible explanations for the U.S. diplomatic move against its European allies. He argues that the United States did not want it to appear as though it was necessary to resort to military action to wield influence in the Middle East because then the Western powers would appear just as brutal as the Soviets. He also asserts that the "president immediately recognized that the Arab world would coalesce [come together] behind Nasser,"[34] thereby making Nasser more powerful at a time when the U.S. goal was

Nasser's Response to the British and French Attack

In a September 15, 1956, speech to the United Arab Republic, President Nasser began by condemning the British and French claims to the Suez Canal, and then proceeded to threaten "those who attack Egypt." The following is an excerpt from that speech as it is found at www.fordham.edu.

Those who attack Egypt will never leave Egypt alive. We shall fight a regular war, a total war, a guerrilla war. Those who attack Egypt will soon realize they brought disaster upon themselves. He who attacks Egypt attacks [the] whole Arab world. They say in their papers the whole thing will be over in forty-eight hours. They do not know how strong we really are.

We believe in international law. But we will never submit. We shall show the world [how] a small country can stand in the face of great powers threatening with armed might. Egypt might be a small power but she is great inasmuch as she has faith in her power and convictions. I feel quite certain every Egyptian shares the same convictions as I do and believes in everything I am stressing now.

We shall defend our freedom and independence to the last drop of our blood. This is the [staunch] feeling of every Egyptian. The whole Arab nation will stand by us in our common fight against aggression and domination. Free peoples, too, people who are really free will stand by us and support us against the forces of tyranny.

Egypt's Port Said lies in ruins following the military attacks of the Suez crisis.

to undermine his influence in the Middle East. According to Takeyh, this U.S. desire to undermine rather than brutally topple Nasser is what led to its anomalous decision to work with the Soviets against its allies to bring about an end to the conflict.

The Eisenhower Doctrine

The British diplomatic defeat in Egypt made one thing abundantly clear—emerging nationalist nations with resources that the superpowers wished to fight over could foil the plans of powerful Western nations such as Great Britain. The importance of emerging nations in the Cold War led American officials to conclude that subsequent battlefronts would involve the "third world" nations of the Middle East, Africa, and Asia.

In Egypt, Nasser continued to gain power following the Suez crisis. To many Arabs, he symbolized their dreams of diminishing Western influence in the Middle East and uniting the Arab peoples. However, the United States viewed him as dangerously allied with the Soviets and tried to ally some of the other Arab nations against him. This was difficult to accomplish since no Arab leader wanted to appear in opposition to Nasser and his Arab nationalism for fear of being attacked by its neighbors. The U.S. solution to this problem came to be called the Eisenhower Doctrine.

In this doctrine, Eisenhower pledged U.S. support to any Middle Eastern nation that found itself under attack from communism. Eisenhower added that this support would be available at any time a leader of a foreign nation requested it. On January 5, 1957, he proposed that Congress should authorize "assistance and cooperation to include the employment of the armed forces of the United States to secure and protect the territorial integrity and political independence of . . . nations, requesting . . . aid, against overt armed aggression from any nation controlled by International Communism."[35]

Previously the United States was committed to containing communism anywhere in the world, but this was done based solely on its own interests—the United States decided where and when it wanted to intervene. Now, the Eisenhower Doctrine stated that the U.S. military could be committed throughout the world at the request of the leader of any foreign nation that was fighting communism. Containment had taken a new turn.

The Eisenhower Doctrine

The following is an excerpt from Eisenhower's "Special Message to the Congress on the situation in the Middle East" given on January 5, 1957. The program it outlines came to be known as the Eisenhower Doctrine. The speech can be found at www.eisenhower.utexas.edu.

The United States through the joint action of the President and the Congress, or, in the case of treaties, the Senate, has manifested in many endangered areas its purpose to support free and independent governments—and peace—against external menace, notably the menace of International Communism. Thereby we have helped to maintain peace and security during a period of great danger. It is now essential that the United States should manifest through joint action of the President and the Congress our determination to assist those nations of the Mid East area, which desire that assistance.

The action which I propose would have the following features.

It would, first of all, authorize the United States to cooperate with and assist any nation or group of nations in the general area of the Middle East in the development of economic strength dedicated to the maintenance of national independence.

It would, in the second place, authorize the Executive to undertake in the same region programs of military assistance and cooperation with any nation or group of nations which desires such aid.

It would, in the third place, authorize such assistance and cooperation to include the employment of the armed forces of the United States to secure and protect the territorial integrity and political independence of such nations, requesting such aid, against overt armed aggression from any nation controlled by International Communism.

Chapter 5

Cuba

In the late 1950s and early 1960s, the United States became entangled in the affairs of a small island nation that lay less than a hundred miles off the coast of Florida—Cuba. The United States became involved in Cuban affairs in an attempt to stop the Soviets from spreading their influence. In so doing, the American government eventually suffered a humiliating loss in the battle to contain communism and found itself on the brink of nuclear war with the Soviets. In fact, all-out nuclear war between the superpowers seemed imminent when for two weeks in October 1962 the two mighty nations pointed weapons of devastation at each other because of a disagreement that began over Cuba.

Cuba and Castro

The United States has a long history of involvement in Cuban domestic affairs. Cuba was granted its independence from Spain in 1898, and the United States quickly came to dominate the small island off its coast by purchasing most of its exports and thereby controlling its economy. The United States also landed troops in Cuba three times during the first half of the twentieth century to stabilize its government.

However, the United States did not intervene in Cuban politics in 1952, when Fulgencio Batista overthrew the constitutionally elected government and began to consolidate power. Batista had formerly served as the Cuban president from 1940 to 1944. When he seized power in 1952, Batista slowly began his evolution into a brutal dictator, sending numerous politicians who opposed him to jail or to their deaths. On July 26, 1953, one such opposition group led by a young rebel named Fidel Castro mounted its first armed attack on the Batista regime. After two failed attempts, in January 1959 Castro's Twenty-Sixth of July Movement succeeded in overthrowing the Batista dictatorship, and Castro assumed power in Cuba.

Castro and the Soviets

In order to complete his revolution, Castro needed help. In April he flew to the United States to request assistance, only to be denied it by the U.S. government. American officials refused to grant Castro aid in part because he had nationalized Cuban lands, which means he seized them from individual landowners and declared they belonged to Cuba (the nation) instead. In the words of Walter LaFeber, "Americans owned 80 percent of Cuba's utilities, 40 percent of its sugar, 90 percent of its mining wealth, and the island's key strategic location of Guantanamo Bay."[36] Therefore, Castro's nationalization of Cuban lands caused many of the Americans who had invested in

Cuba to lose a great deal of money. In addition, this structure of land ownership is also fundamental to communism, and therefore the United States grew wary of Castro's intentions.

Castro had nationalized the land because he wanted Cuba to be more independent and less reliant on the United States. As it became clear that this would only anger the Americans, Castro turned to the Soviets. To assist Castro, the Soviets sent well over a hundred advisers from the Soviet security and intelligence agency,

Cuban leader Fidel Castro (center left) arrives in New York in 1959. After assuming power in Cuba, Castro sought assistance from the United States but was denied.

called the KGB, to bolster his intelligence and security systems. Less than a year later, the Soviet Union formally recognized Castro's regime as the official government of Cuba.

In an odd twist of U.S. containment policy, the United States deliberately tried to push Castro toward communism. P.M.H. Bell explains:

> this was done "in the belief that this would render [Castro's regime] unpopular [in Cuba] and so bring about its fall. . . . This elaborate policy succeeded to a point, in that the regime became more radical and developed ties with the Soviet Union; but it failed completely in its main objective."[37]

The United States had miscalculated, and Cuba's alignment with the Soviets did not make Castro unpopular in Cuba and lead to his overthrow. Thus, the United States had accidentally assisted in the creation of a Cuban state with strong ties to the Soviets.

The Bay of Pigs Invasion

Now the Eisenhower administration had to contain the communism that brewed just ninety miles off U.S. shores, and therefore decided to impose economic sanctions on Cuba. Sanctions are restrictions put on a nation to force it to comply with another nation's demands. In this case, the United States wanted Castro out of power and hoped that refusing to buy goods from Cuba would cause so much economic despair that Castro would either give up power willingly or be overthrown. However, with the support of the Soviets, such sanctions had very little effect on the Cuban economy except to give the Soviets more control over it. By the end of 1961, 80 percent of Cuban trade was done with the Soviet bloc—the Soviet Union and its satellites.

President Eisenhower then decided to try eradicating communism in Cuba by getting rid of Castro himself. Since it would look bad for an American president to appear as though he was trying to oust another world leader, Eisenhower enlisted the CIA to arrange a covert method to eliminate the Cuban leader. This way, once Castro was out of power, the president could deny any U.S. involvement in the affair.

After a few attempts to assassinate Castro failed, the CIA began working on a plan to assist anti-Castro forces in a full-scale invasion of Cuba to remove the leader from power. The planning and preparations for a covert action code-named Operation Pluto were underway. The goal was to locate a rebel leader who would see eye to eye with the United States and assist him in mounting a paramilitary attack to seize power in Cuba—or, in reality, mount that invasion for him.

The search for a fitting rebel leader began and was quite difficult, since Castro had wiped out most of his opponents after seizing power. In the absence of a

The Bay of Pigs Plan

The following is an excerpt from the CIA plan, "A Program of Covert Action Against the Castro Regime," which President Eisenhower authorized in March 1960. The plan calls for the measures that were eventually taken to try to oust Castro in the disastrous Bay of Pigs invasion. It can be found at www.parascope.com.

2. Summary Outline: The program contemplates four major courses of action:

a) The first requirement is the creation of a responsible, appealing and unified Cuban opposition to the Castro regime, publicly declared as such and therefore necessarily located outside of Cuba. It is hoped that within one month a political entity can be formed in the shape of a council or junta, through the merger of three acceptable opposition groups. . . . The council will be encouraged to adopt as its slogan "Restore the Revolution". . . .

d) Preparations have already been made for the development of an adequate paramilitary force outside Cuba. . . . Initially a cadre of leaders will be recruited. . . . In a second phase a number of paramilitary cadres will be trained at a secure location outside of the U.S. so as to be available for immediate deployment into Cuba. . . . In the meanwhile, a limited air capability for resupply and for infiltration and exfiltration already exists under CIA control.

legitimate leader of an existing group, the CIA worked to formulate one. Eventually, they were able to align five exiled Cuban leaders to form the Cuban Democratic Revolutionary Front (FRD, or Frente Revolucionario Democrático).

The CIA set up a base in Guatemala called Camp Trax to offer paramilitary training to this new rebel group. Here the recruits were given weapons, taught how to use them, and trained in paramilitary action by CIA contract employees. While ground forces were being trained, the CIA also created an air force and a navy for the rebels. By the time of the invasion, the rebels had thousands of soldiers, roughly thirty U.S. planes, and two World War II vessels. In arranging all of this, the CIA had to make it look as though the FRD was doing the planning and the U.S. had no hand in the operation.

In the end this proved to be impossible, and the invasion itself was a complete disaster. President Kennedy, who had taken office just three months before and given the go-ahead for the invasion, was humiliated both domestically and internationally. While the CIA had successfully assembled forces, it had not provided good intelligence reports, especially about the capabilities of Castro's forces. When the CIA's twelve hundred exiled Cubans tried to set up a beachhead in an area known as the Bay of Pigs on April 17, 1961, Castro was ready for the assault. By April 18 the President's Assistant for National Security Affairs, McGeorge Bundy, was informing Kennedy that "The Cuban armed forces

Cuban soldiers display a bloodstained shirt worn by an FRD solider killed in the ill-fated Bay of Pigs invasion in 1961.

are stronger, the popular [support of the invasion] is weaker, and our tactical position is feebler than we had hoped. Tanks have done in one beachhead, and the position is precarious at the others."[38] In the end, Castro's forces defeated the rebel forces in less than three days' time.

The Aftermath

Asked to ascertain Western European nations' reactions to the Bay of Pigs,

Kennedy's Special Assistant Arthur Schlesinger reported on May 3, 1961, that he "encountered everywhere what can only be described as a hunger for a rational explanation of the Cuban operation. . . . The available stories had left most people baffled and incredulous. They could not believe that the U.S. Government had been quite so incompetent, irresponsible and stupid as the bare facts of the operation suggested."[39]

On May 1, 1961, Castro publicly declared Cuba a socialist state. In the ideology of communism, socialism is a stage in the evolution of a state that follows capitalism and precedes communism. Thus, Castro was declaring his nation on the path to communism. In his speech, Castro added there was no need for elections since the overwhelming majority supported him. For the first time in its many attempts to contain communism around the globe, the United States had completely lost a battle. Worse yet, it had lost a battle just ninety miles off its own coast. In addition, the United States had been humiliated, as British, French, and American newspaper publishers and editors wondered why a superpower such as the United States found Cuba to be such a big threat. In the words of Schlesinger, Cuba had made the U.S. government look "self-righteous, trigger-happy and incompetent"[40] in the eyes of the press.

Furious that the Cuban dictator had bested him, Kennedy moved to get rid of Castro once again, and to these ends he initiated Operation Mongoose, which was designed to "help the people of Cuba overthrow the Communist regime from within Cuba and institute a new government with which the United States can live in peace."[41] The operation included some serious attempts to disperse propaganda in Cuba and sabotage the sugar crop. However, it also included plots to poison Castro's cigars and doctor photographs to make him appear to be a fat gigolo. In the end, little came of Operation Mongoose.

The Cuban Missile Crisis Begins

The Soviets now had an ally in Cuba, and they began to use it. As summer turned to fall, the CIA began to hear stories from Cuban refugees about Russian rockets on flatbed trucks, and it became increasingly more suspicious about the bases the Soviets were building in Cuba. Based on these

---

CIA Plots Against the Castro Regime

The CIA was frequently devising plots to disrupt or overthrow the Castro Regime. On February 2, 1962, Brigadier General William Craig sent this memo to Brig. General Edward Lansdale. Lansdale was the commander of the Kennedy administration's "Operation Mongoose," a covert action program designed to do anything and everything to get rid of Castro. The document lists plans to "provoke, harass, or disrupt" the government of Fidel Castro. Two of these plans are detailed below. The document can be found at www.parascope.com.

2. Operation FREE RIDE:

a. *Objective:* The objective is to create unrest and dissension amongst the Cuban people.

b. *Concept:* This is to be accomplished by airdropping valid Pan American or KLM one-way airline tickets good for passage to Mexico City, Caracas, etc. (none to the U.S.). Tickets could be intermixed with other leaflets planned to be dropped. The number of tickets dropped could be increased. The validity of the tickets would have to be restricted to a time period.

11. Operation GOOD TIMES:

a. *Objective:* To disillusion the Cuban population with Castro's image by distribution of fake photographic material.

b. *Concept:* Prepare a desired photograph, such as an obese Castro with two beauties in any situation desired, ostensibly within a room in the Castro residence, lavishly furnished, and a table brimming over with the most delectable Cuban food with an underlying caption (appropriately Cuban) such as 'My ration is different.' Make as many prints as desired on sterile paper and then distribute over the countryside by air drops or agents. This should put even a Commie Dictator in the proper perspective with the underprivileged masses.

suspicions, the CIA used aerial reconnaissance (the use of aircraft to gather information for military purposes) to ascertain what military equipment was being shipped from the Soviet Union to Cuba throughout the summer of 1962. Then on October 14, U-2 spy planes equipped with photoreconnaissance capabilities obtained photographic evidence of Soviet medium range nuclear

U.S. Ambassador Adlai Stevenson (far right) explains aerial photographs of Cuban missile sites (below) to the UN Security Council in 1962.

missiles in Cuba. At first, the USSR denied the presence of nuclear missiles in Cuba but confirmed their presence after being confronted on the floor of the United Nations with photographic evidence from the U-2 spy plane.

President Kennedy saw the presence of these warheads in Cuba as further disruption of the balance of power in favor of communism and a significant physical threat to the safety of the United States. If the United States allowed the Soviets to intrude without consequence into what had always been seen as the U.S. sphere of interest, some officials wondered where the intrusion would stop. After a week of closed-door meetings with his advisers to discuss the best course of action, Kennedy decided to enact a naval blockade. The blockade was a show of force since American naval capability far exceeded that of the Soviets. However, it was not directly confrontational and therefore allowed the Soviets an out. Kennedy added that, as an immediate first step, the United States would impose a naval quarantine, in which all vessels approaching Cuba would be stopped, searched, and if "found to contain cargoes of offensive weapons,"[42] promptly turned back.

Over the course of the next fourteen days, the two superpowers stood on the brink of nuclear war. In an October 22 television broadcast, Kennedy broke the news to the American public. He told listeners, "unmistakable evidence has established the fact that a series of offensive missile sites is now in preparation [in Cuba]. The purpose of these bases can be none other than to provide a nuclear strike capability against the Western Hemisphere."[43] He also demanded the removal of the missiles and made it clear that any missile launched from Cuba would be seen as "an attack by the Soviet Union on the United States, requiring a full retaliatory response upon the Soviet Union."[44]

That same day, Kennedy wrote to Soviet Premier Nikita Khrushchev reiterating the fact that "the United States could not tolerate any action on [the part of the Soviets] which in a major way disturbed the existing over-all balance of power in the world." Kennedy vowed that the "United States would do whatever must be done to protect its own security and that of its allies."[45] At the time, this meant proceeding with the quarantine while debating other options.

Khrushchev responded in a telegram stating the quarantine was illegal according to international laws that guaranteed the freedom to navigate the high seas. He added that Kennedy's actions were bound to "lead to catastrophic consequences for peace throughout world."[46] Kennedy responded to this telegram informing Khrushchev that the quarantine would proceed. "I hope that you will issue immediately the necessary instructions to your ships to observe the terms of the quarantine," Kennedy added, "which will go into effect at 1400 hours Greenwich time October twenty-four."[47]

Soviet Missiles in Cuba Announced by President Kennedy

On October 22, 1962, President John F. Kennedy went on national television to announce the presence of Soviet nuclear missiles in Cuba. At the same time, Kennedy announced actions being taken by the United States to quarantine further offensive military equipment and keep it from entering Cuba. The following is an excerpt from the speech. It can be found at www.mtholyoke.edu.

Acting, therefore, in the defense of our own security and of the entire Western Hemisphere, and under the authority entrusted to me by the Constitution as endorsed by the Resolution of the Congress, I have directed that the following *initial* steps be taken immediately:

First: To halt this offensive buildup, a strict quarantine on all offensive military equipment under shipment to Cuba is being initiated. All ships of any kind bound for Cuba from whatever nation or port will, if found to contain cargoes of offensive weapons, be turned back. This quarantine will be extended, if needed, to other types of cargo and carriers. . . .

Third: It shall be the policy of this Nation to regard any nuclear missile launched from Cuba against any nation in the Western Hemisphere as an attack by the Soviet Union on the United States, requiring a full retaliatory response upon the Soviet Union. . . .

Seventh and finally: I call upon Chairman Khrushchev to halt and eliminate this clandestine, reckless, and provocative threat to world peace and to stable relations between our two nations. I call upon him further to abandon this course of world domination, and to join in an historic effort to end the perilous arms race and to transform the history of man. He has an opportunity now to move the world back from the abyss of destruction—by returning to his government's own words that it had no need to station missiles outside its own territory, and withdrawing these weapons from Cuba—by refraining from any action which will widen or deepen the present crisis—and then by participating in a search for peaceful and permanent solutions.

President Kennedy announces on national television the presence of Soviet nuclear missiles in Cuba.

A Solution to the Crisis

The days that followed were the most nerve-racking days of the entire Cold War. U.S. troops were massing in Florida, the nuclear missile sites in Cuba were approaching completion, and ships bound for Cuba carrying nuclear warheads were approaching the blockade. The world watched tensely as the first Soviet vessel approached the blockade wondering whether this was the beginning of World War III and mass nuclear destruction. Finally, after tense moments when the Soviet vessels carrying offensive weapons reached the blockade, they turned around and headed back from whence they came. Khrushchev had chosen not to directly confront the United States. Journalist Richard Reeves lends insight into Khrushchev's actions in a 1997 article about the Cuban missile crisis. Reeves writes, "according to Soviet historians, Khrushchev said: 'We are face to face with the danger of war and nuclear catastrophe. In order to save the world we must retreat.'"[48]

However, the quarantine provided only a temporary solution to the problem, since it stopped the delivery of any more nuclear missiles but did nothing to get rid of the nuclear warheads already in Cuba. On October 26, Khrushchev made the first move toward resolution of the conflict. In a long letter that discussed the horrors of nuclear war, Khrushchev stated that if the United States would promise not to attack Cuba, the Soviets would remove their missiles from that nation. A second letter arrived later that day that also requested the United States to remove its Jupiter missiles from Turkey, which posed a threat to the USSR similar to that which medium range missiles in Cuba posed to the United States. The United States agreed on both accounts, and the world breathed a sigh of relief as the superpowers moved back from the brink of nuclear war. Never before in the course of human history had such mass destruction been contemplated, and the United States and the USSR never again came so close to nuclear war. While it could be argued that the United States had succeeded in stopping the spread of communism on this day, when all was said and done, both superpowers were happy to call it a draw and relieved that the nuclear standoff was over.

Chapter 6

Vietnam

I n 1950 the U.S. involvement in Vietnam began. This particular foreign entanglement would eventually prove to be the longest and most costly U.S. commitment during the Cold War. The American fight to stop communism from spreading into South Vietnam spanned more than two decades and involved the foreign policy decisions of six presidents. As the Vietnam conflict escalated, the United States increased the commitment of American resources and troops. However, in early 1968 U.S. officials began to question whether the war in Vietnam could be won. For the first time in Cold War history they reined in containment policy, making it applicable to fewer situations instead of more and decreasing the U.S. commitment to fight communism around the globe.

Early Involvement

The struggle for power in Vietnam began as soon as World War II ended. The whole of Vietnam had been a French colony before the war, but at war's end, the Vietnamese nationalist Ho Chi Minh proclaimed himself the leader of a provisional government in the North Vietnamese city of Hanoi. The French controlled the South, and both parties fought to gain control over all of Vietnam. By the end of 1950, Ho Chi Minh had declared the Democratic Republic of Vietnam in the North, which the USSR, Yugoslavia, and China promptly recognized. Ho Chi Minh's alignment with the Soviets caused U.S. officials to see his regime as Communist and part of a Soviet master plan to take over Southeast Asia. Therefore, the United States and Great Britain threw their support behind the pro-Western, French-supported government of Bao Dai in South Vietnam.

However, U.S. support did not end there. President Truman also gave the French financial backing and military equipment. On May 8, 1950, the secretary of state made the following statement:

> The United States Government, convinced that neither national independence nor democratic evolution exist in any area dominated by Soviet imperialism, considers the situation [in Vietnam] to be such as to warrant. . .

Ho Chi Minh (second from right) declared himself leader of North Vietnam following WWII.

economic aid and military equipment to [Dai's government in South Vietnam] and to France in order to assist them in restoring stability and permitting these states to pursue their peaceful and democratic development.[49]

This marked the beginning of U.S. economic and military involvement in Vietnam. Over the next four years, the United States sent upwards of $1.2 billion in aid to the French—by 1954, 70 percent of France's military budget was paid by the Americans.

Eisenhower's Domino Theory

The battle between the French forces and those of Ho Chi Minh escalated, culminating in a battle at Dien Bien Phu, which began on March 13, 1954. When it became clear the French could not win without assistance, President Eisenhower surmised that the United States needed to deepen its commitment in Vietnam. In his opinion, the time had come to send in American troops, not just money and equipment. Eisenhower asked Congress to commit troops to come to the aid of the French. His justification for this commitment was based

French legionnaires question a North Vietnamese soldier in 1954.

on his now famous "domino theory." At a news conference on April 6, 1954, he described a scenario in which the "fall" of French Indochina (the present-day states of Vietnam, Laos, and Cambodia) to communism would lead to the loss of Burma, Thailand, the whole Indochina Peninsula, and Indonesia. The loss of these nations to communism would then threaten Japan, Formosa (Taiwan), the Philippines, and the Marianas, as well as Australia and New Zealand.

Thus, in Eisenhower's opinion, since dominoes gained momentum as they fell and the last fell much more quickly than the first, it was the job of the United States to halt Communist aggression at its beginning. In this analogy, Vietnam was the first domino. If it were knocked over, it would eventually leave Japan unprotected in the face of Russian and Chinese expansion, and Japan was the key to containing communism in the East. Therefore, when it became apparent that the French were destined to lose the war in Vietnam, Eisenhower hinted to congressional leaders that he would like to be allowed to commit U.S. forces to the region.

His request was denied for political reasons (mainly that the Joint Chiefs of Staff were split on the matter), and on May 7, 1954, the French were forced to surrender at Dien Bien Phu. In the subsequent settlement, called the Geneva Accords, Vietnam was split into north and south along the seventeenth parallel with Ho Chi Minh's forces in North Vietnam and the French in the south. A general election was to be held in two years that would unify Vietnam under one leader.

The French were to remain in Saigon to help carry out these elections before withdrawing all their troops.

The United States Takes up the Torch

It appeared as though the fighting was over and whichever regime would come to power in Vietnam would do so through the national elections. However, as the French withdrew, the United States increased its economic involvement in Vietnam because American officials hoped to sway the upcoming elections in favor of the anti-Communist forces of the south. Thus, less than two months after the French gave up their claim to Vietnam, the United States began directly funding the South Vietnamese government and sending military advisers to train the South Vietnamese armed forces.

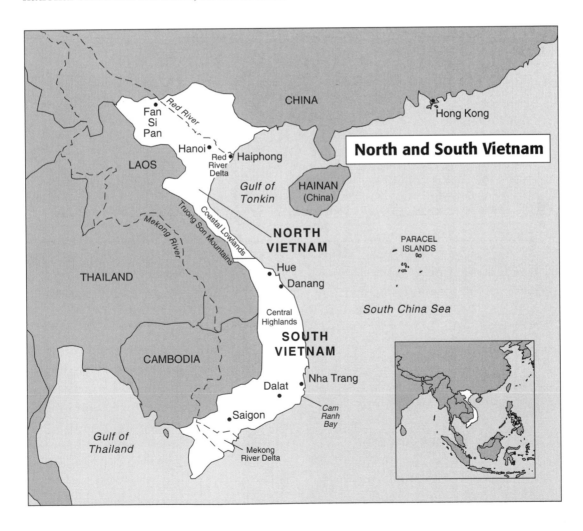

North and South Vietnam

Citing the domino theory, U.S. officials did everything in their power to stop Ho Chi Minh from taking control of a united Vietnam. They realized that Ho Chi Minh would easily win any election. As Eisenhower states in his book, *Mandate for Change,* he was absolutely certain that Ho Chi Minh would have prevailed in 1954:

> I have never talked or corresponded with a person knowledgeable in Indochinese affairs who did not agree that had elections been held as of the time of the fighting [between the French and Ho Chi Minh's forces], possibly 80 per cent of the population would have voted for the Communist Ho Chi Minh as their leader.[50]

In 1956 Eisenhower seems to have believed that little had changed, and rather than risk losing all of Vietnam to the Communists, the U.S. government was content to back Diem's refusal to hold the elections required by the Geneva Accords and thereby maintain the status quo—a divided Vietnam.

Kennedy Forges Ahead

Thus, the United States supported the continued division of Vietnam and provided economic aid and military equip-

U.S. military advisors teach South Vietnamese soldiers how to use a grenade launcher.

ment to South Vietnamese forces during the Eisenhower presidency. When Eisenhower's successor, John F. Kennedy, took office, he deepened this commitment. When asked why his brother saw fit to intervene in Vietnam, Robert F. Kennedy told historian John Martin that his brother believed "the loss of all of Southeast Asia [would come] if you lost Vietnam. I think everybody was quite clear that the rest of Southeast Asia would fall."[51]

While this belief in the domino theory was an important part of Kennedy's decision to increase U.S. commitment in Vietnam, his decision was also influenced by a number of other factors. Chief among them was Kennedy's conviction that he needed to reestablish the international credibility of the United States after the Bay of Pigs debacle. Shortly after the American defeat in Cuba, Kennedy confided to James Reston of *The New York Times* that "Now we have a problem in making our power credible, and Vietnam is the place [to prove that it is]."[52]

Believing the ramifications of losing Vietnam would be severe and wanting to reestablish U.S. authority abroad, Kennedy sent Vice President Lyndon B. Johnson on a fact-finding mission to Vietnam in May 1961 and General Maxwell Taylor and Walt Whitman Rostrow on a similar mission in October. Upon returning to the United States, the Taylor-Rostrow team recommended Kennedy increase the number of U.S. military advisers in Vietnam.

An American soldier (right) explains helicopter airlift procedures to Vietnamese infantrymen in 1962.

After examining the options, Kennedy eventually decided to increase the number of U.S. military advisers in Vietnam from three thousand to nine thousand men by the end of 1962. In addition to the commitment of more American personnel, these advisers also were being asked to play an increasingly military role in the conflict. The lines were blurring between advice and combat, as a good number of these advisers engaged in actual fighting. At the same time, the president also dedicated some of the U.S. air forces to make air strikes against Communist strongholds in South Vietnam. Over the course of a year of Kennedy's presidency, the United States had gone from being a financial backer and supplier of military equipment to South Vietnamese forces to sending in "advisers" to engage in combat and using its air force to support the southern military effort.

Once Kennedy had reestablished U.S. credibility by containing communism in places around the world other than Vietnam (such as Berlin during the Berlin Crisis), he still remained committed to an increased American role in the Vietnam conflict. This was due, in part, to the fact that his administration felt it had discovered the secret to stopping communism. In the words of Walter LaFeber, the administration believed "it knew how to threaten to apply or, if necessary, actually apply conventional military power to obtain maximum results."[53]

This overconfidence in the American ability to contain communism through the application of just the right amount of conventional warfare led Kennedy to commit more and more U.S. troops to the South Vietnamese cause in the war. As a result, by the end of 1963 fifteen thousand American advisers were operating in Vietnam, and the United States provided $500 million in aid to the South Vietnamese over the course of that year.

Johnson Takes the Helm

On November 22, 1963, John F. Kennedy was assassinated, and Lyndon B. Johnson became president of the United States. Under Johnson's reign, the U.S. commitment in Vietnam would increase to unprecedented levels. Johnson's approach was slightly different from his predecessors'. While Kennedy, Eisenhower, and Truman had refused to withdraw from Vietnam but balked at engaging in a large-scale conflict, Johnson announced that he was out to win the war. In 1965 Johnson made it clear that he was committed to sending U.S. troops to Vietnam until victory was achieved. "America wins the wars that she undertakes," he said. "Make no mistake about it."[54]

In combination with his desire to win, Johnson soon garnered unprecedented power to wage war in Vietnam. This came as the result of an August 2, 1964, attack in the Gulf of Tonkin bordered by North Vietnam and China. On this day, and again on August 4, North Vietnamese torpedo boats attacked a U.S. destroyer

The Gulf of Tonkin Resolution

On two separate days in early August 1964, North Vietnamese torpedo boats attacked a U.S. destroyer named the *Maddox*. In the wake of this attack, President Johnson asked Congress to grant him unlimited power to wage the war in Vietnam. Congress obliged when they passed the Gulf of Tonkin Resolution, a portion of which appears below and can be found at the American Civil Rights Review's Document Archive at http://webusers.anet-stl.com.

Resolved by the Senate and House of Representatives of the United States of America in Congress assembled, That the Congress approves and supports the determination of the President, as Commander in Chief, to take all necessary measures to repel any armed attack against the forces of the United States and to prevent further aggression.

Sec. 2. The United States regards as vital to its national interest and to world peace the maintenance of international peace and security in southeast Asia. Consonant with the Constitution of the United States and the Charter of the United Nations and in accordance with its obligations under the Southeast Asia Collective Defense Treaty, the United States is, therefore, prepared, as the President determines, to take all necessary steps, including the use of armed force, to assist any member or protocol state of the Southeast Asia Collective Defense Treaty requesting assistance in defense of its freedom.

Sec. 3. This resolution shall expire when the President shall determine that the peace and security of the area is reasonably assured by international conditions created by action of the United Nations or otherwise, except that it may be terminated earlier by concurrent resolution of the Congress.

President Johnson (seated) signs the Gulf of Tonkin Resolution in 1964.

Voices From Vietnam

On February 8, 1965, President Lyndon Johnson ordered the twenty thousand American military advisers in Vietnam to transform themselves into combatants. Concurrent with this order JeDon A. Emenhiser surveyed the opinions of a sample of the more than 4,100 civilian and military personnel stationed in the Saigon area. His findings were released in his paper, "Voices from Americans in VietNam, February, 1965," which was presented to the 24th Annual Meeting of the Popular Culture Association on April 6, 1994. Below is the response of one interviewee. The paper can be found at http://sorrel.humboldt.edu.

A member of the Air Force from the Southwest . . . said: . . . "I don't believe the U.S. is benefiting the people of VietNam. I'm willing to wager that the amount of U.S. money being poured into VietNam is what is causing the downfall of so many governments in Saigon. All the different factions are engaged in a struggle to get into power where they can get control of the majority of these funds for their own use. The common people of VietNam want nothing more than to be left alone. Most of them believe they can exist peacefully under communism. As long as they hold that belief anything done by the U.S. to make them fight is resented; and the U.S., in their eyes, becomes the imperialist aggressor. Now is this benefiting them or us? Until the people themselves want to fight communism—we're spinning our wheels."

named the *Maddox* (although there is some debate as to whether the United States precipitated the attack.)

In response to the situation, Congress passed the Gulf of Tonkin Resolution at President Johnson's request. The resolution gave him the power "to take all necessary measures to repel any armed attack against the forces of the United States and to prevent further aggression."[55] Johnson promptly deepened America's commitment to the war in Vietnam—by the end of 1965, two hundred thousand U.S. troops were stationed in Vietnam, and a year later that number had doubled.

The Tet Offensive

Over the next four years Johnson continued to increase American involvement in the war, and by the end of 1967, more than half a million U.S. soldiers were in Vietnam. Johnson also continued to expand the role of U.S. forces. In April 1965 he called upon the U.S. Air Force to begin Operation Rolling Thunder, a bombing campaign in North Vietnam. (Previously, U.S. bombing of targets had been limited to the strongholds of the Vietcong, a Communist-led guerilla force in South Vietnam.)

The Americans continued to dedicate more and more troops to containing communism in Vietnam until February 1968 when the North Vietnamese launched an all-out offensive on the Buddhist holiday of Tet (New Year). Catching their opponents completely off guard, the Vietcong were able to capture parts of the South

Vietnamese capital of Saigon and even fight their way into the U.S. embassy compound there. While the U.S. and South Vietnamese forces eventually regrouped and claimed a military victory in the battle, the Tet Offensive called into question Johnson's actions as well as his decision to entangle the United States so deeply in Vietnamese affairs.

Prior to Tet, there had been a great deal of disagreement between the CIA

American tanks advance on Saigon in 1966 (top). A Vietnamese civilian awaits medical attention (above).

and military intelligence as to the size of Communist forces. The army estimated three hundred thousand Communists, the CIA twice that. Taking the army's estimates, it appeared as though the United States might be nearing victory. Johnson had taken these numbers and made reassurances to the American people that the end was in sight. However, the sheer

The Tet Offensive

Myron Harrington who commanded a hundred-man company during the Tet Offensive recalls the situation in Hué. The passage is reprinted as it is found in Stanley Karnow's *Vietnam: A History.*

As a marine, I had to admire the courage and discipline of the North Vietnamese and Vietcong, but no more than I did my own men. We were both in a face-to-face, eyeball-to-eyeball confrontation. Sometimes they were only twenty or thirty yards from us, and once we killed a sniper only ten yards away. After a while, survival was the name of the game as you sat there in the semidarkness, with the firing going on constantly, like at a rifle range. And the horrible smell. You tasted it as you ate your rations, as if you were eating death. It permeated your clothes, which you couldn't wash because water was very scarce. You couldn't bathe or shave either. My strategy was to keep as many of my marines alive as possible, and yet accomplish our mission. You went through the full range of emotions, seeing your buddies being hit, but you couldn't feel sorry for them because you had the other to think about. It was dreary, and still we weren't depressed. We were doing our job—successfully.

numbers of North Vietnamese killed or wounded during the Tet Offensive proved that the CIA's numbers were closer to the mark and that the Vietnamese conflict was nowhere near its end.

Historian Nathan Miller explains the effect this had on Johnson's presidency:

[While it was a military victory] . . . the battle appeared different on the color television screens in American living rooms. The chaotic images—Vietcong swarming into the embassy grounds, wounded and dead strewn about the streets, buildings shelled, huts in flames, refugees fleeing, women wailing in anguish—did not convey a sense of triumph. . . . Having been repeatedly assured by the president that "there was a light at the end of the tunnel" in Vietnam, most Americans were shocked by the bloody spectacle. The major casualty of Tet proved to be public faith in Johnson's credibility.[56]

Antiwar sentiment in the United States increased, and elected officials who had previously supported the increased commitment of U.S. forces to contain communism in Vietnam now began to look for a way out.

In a March 31, 1968, television broadcast, President Johnson retreated from his earlier position that America would stay in the war until it was won. Instead, he announced that he was ordering an end to the bombing of North Vietnam

Bodies of Vietcong fighters litter the street after the Tet Offensive. Americans were shocked by the violence of the 1968 attack.

and initiating peace talks. After eighteen years in which the United States steadily increased its involvement in Vietnam to contain communism, Johnson made the first move to decrease the American role. For the first time, the U.S. military had lost a war.

The New Face of Containment

As they departed Vietnam, American troops left behind a country in which the United States had failed to meet its objective of containing communism despite outright military involvement. As a result, the free rein that President Johnson was given to wage war in Vietnam was called into question, and containment policy was forced to evolve once again to meet the challenges of a United States faced with a very different set of circumstances. At this time, containment shifted course. Whereas previous administrations had expanded containment to include more and more areas around the world, the United States now altered its policy to include the defense of fewer nations from the Communist threat.

This was due, in part, to the fact that the position of the United States in the international community had changed. When Truman first involved the United States in the affairs of Vietnam to contain communism, the United States was the most powerful nation in the world. The same was true when Eisenhower sent troops to safeguard South Korea and when Kennedy faced off with Khrushchev in the missile crisis. In fact, an essential component of containment was being more powerful than the Soviets. The drain of the Vietnam War on the U.S. military and economy, coupled with a Soviet military buildup, significantly undermined the dominance of the United States in the world.

This was the world that Richard M. Nixon faced when he became president in 1968. Realizing that the United States no longer necessarily had the power— or the American public's backing—to contain communism anywhere it might

President Nixon visits American troops in Vietnam in 1969.

arise, he moved away from the open-ended commitments of his predecessors to stop communism everywhere and began to "manage" it instead. Walter LaFeber explains:

Containment was as important in the 1970s as the late 1940s, but because of the new Russian strength, and the relative decline of American power, containment now had to be constructed differently than when Acheson or John Kennedy made policy. Nixon . . . believed the Soviets could be contained not by a massive arms race or increased United States global commitments . . . but by making a deal: the Soviets could have sorely needed economic help if they cooperated in Vietnam and agreed to arms limitations.[57]

In other words, Nixon strove to contain the Soviets not by a show of force but by offering them incentives to halt expansion.

The Nixon Doctrine and Vietnamization

Nixon laid out a new approach to containment in his November 3, 1969, speech to the nation. In what came to be known as the Nixon Doctrine, he advocated limiting the circumstances under which the United States would intervene to contain Communist aggression. Nixon told listeners the United States would come to a nation's aid only under the following circumstances: 1) if the United States had signed a treaty to come to a given country's

The Nixon Doctrine

In a November 3, 1969, speech to the American people, Nixon outlined what came to be known as the Nixon Doctrine, which described the "Vietnamization" of Vietnam. An excerpt of the speech appears below, and the speech can be found in its entirety at http://oll.temple.edu.

> We Americans are a do-it-yourself people. We are an impatient people.
>
> Instead of teaching someone else to do a job, we like to do it ourselves. And this trait has been carried over into our foreign policy.
>
> In Korea and again in Vietnam, the United States furnished most of the money, most of the arms, and most of the men to help the people of those countries defend their freedom against Communist aggression.
>
> Before any American troops were committed to Vietnam, a leader of another Asian country expressed this opinion to me when I was traveling in Asia as a private citizen.

He said: "When you are trying to assist another nation defend its freedom, U.S. policy should be to help them fight the war but not to fight the war for them." . . .

Well, in accordance with this wise counsel, I laid down in Guam three principles as guidelines for future American policy toward Asia:

— First, the United States will keep all of its treaty commitments.

— Second, we shall provide a shield if a nuclear power threatens the freedom of a nation allied with us or of a nation whose survival we consider vital to our security.

— Third, in cases involving other types of aggression, we shall furnish military and economic assistance when requested in accordance with our treaty commitments. But we shall look to the nation directly threatened to assume the primary responsibility of providing the manpower for its defense.

aid, 2) if a nuclear power threatened an ally or a nation vital to U.S. security. As for those nations that might come under attack by nonnuclear powers, the United States would "furnish military and economic assistance when requested in accordance with our treaty commitments. But . . . look to the nation directly threatened to assume the primary responsibility of providing the manpower for its defense."[58]

In line with this doctrine, Nixon sought to bring American troops home from Vietnam and leave the people of South Vietnam to assume the "responsibility of providing the manpower" for the defense of their nation. Thus, the president sought to decrease the U.S. commitment by providing training to build up the South Vietnamese army while beginning the phased withdrawal of American combat troops. The newly trained Vietnamese recruits would replace the departing American troops, as promised. This program was called the "Vietnamization" of South Vietnamese forces.

Vietnamization did not work out very well in practice. The phased withdrawal of U.S. troops began in 1969, but the war continued for roughly four more years. In fact, in 1972, three years after Vietnamization began and the war was supposedly winding down, more than twenty thousand U.S. soldiers were killed in Vietnam. Finally, in February 1973, the Americans and the North and South Vietnamese concluded a peace treaty to bring about the close of the longest war in U.S. history. The Americans had been involved in the war in one way or another for more than two decades—so much so, in fact, that the Vietnamese people call this war the American War. In this time, U.S. containment policy had shifted significantly from a doctrine that sought to fight communism anywhere it might arise in the world to one which vowed to stop its spread only under very specific circumstances.

Chapter 7

Angola

The United States and the Soviet Union brought the Cold War to Africa by jockeying for influence in the southwest African nation of Angola. The two superpowers had learned several lessons about how important emerging nations could be to their respective causes. So in 1974, when the colonial power of Portugal announced it would withdraw from Angola in November 1975, both the United States and the USSR saw it as a chance to gain a new ally in the Cold War. In the case of the United States, which had just suffered a devastating loss in Vietnam, stopping Communists from coming to power in Angola seemed even more important, since doing so would show the world that the Americans still had the power to contain communism.

The Anticolonial and Portuguese Forces

U.S. involvement in Angola began in the early 1960s. After more than half a century of external colonial rule, Angolan nationalist groups began to engage in guerilla warfare against their Portuguese colonizers in the anticolonial war in 1961. Eventually, three primary rebel groups emerged: the National Front for the Liberation of Angola (FNLA), founded by Holden Roberto in 1954; the Popular Movement for the Liberation of Angola (MPLA), which had close ties to the Angolan Communist Party; and the National Union for the Total Independence of Angola (UNITA), founded in 1966 by Roberto's chief lieutenant, Jonas Savimbi, who broke off from the FNLA to form his own group. Each of these three groups created its own armed forces, which battled the Portuguese army that occupied Angola.

As these rebel groups faced off against the Portuguese military, the United States once again found itself caught between a colonial power it could not afford to anger and a nationalist group it wished to

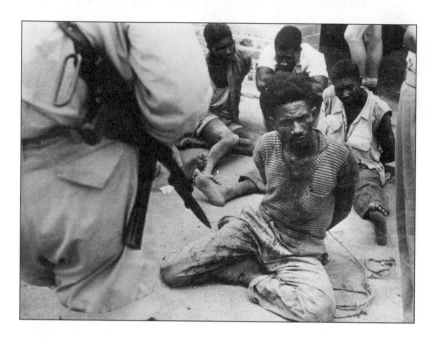

Angolan rebels await sentencing by Portuguese officials in 1955. The Portuguese occupied Angola until 1975.

court. Portugal was under the leadership of the dictator Antonio de Oliveira Salazar and wished to retain absolute control over its African colonies. The United States could not risk angering the Portuguese, because every year it had to renegotiate a lease for air and naval bases in the Azores islands, which were part of Portugal. These bases in the mid-Atlantic were extremely important for the deployment of U.S. troops to Europe and therefore seen as crucial for protecting Europe from the Soviets in the Cold War. The United States had to remain on good terms with Portugal to have access to this strategic defensive position, which in turn

greatly influenced all U.S. policies toward Portugal and, consequently, its colony of Angola in the 1960s and early 1970s.

A Political Tightrope

As a result, the United States had to walk a political tightrope between Portugal and the Angolans. American officials could not anger the Portuguese, but they also realized the pivotal role that the emerging nation of Angola might come to play in African politics and wanted to make certain that they—and not the Soviets—influenced the developing nation. In the early 1960s the Kennedy administration decided to err on the side of the anticolonialist forces in Angola and risk angering the Portuguese.

The United States showed its support for the rebels' cause by voting for a number of resolutions in the United Nations General Assembly as well as the Security Council. This included a resolution that "condemned Portugal's repression of the uprisings in Angola."[59] In addition to this diplomatic support for the Angolan anticolonialists, the United States also provided some funding. The Kennedy administration authorized financial support to Roberto's budding FNLA movement in

1961. Because funding had to be funneled covertly through the CIA so that Portugal would not know of U.S. actions, the facts of U.S. support are difficult to determine. Estimates for the first year of funding alone have a wide range, somewhere between $10,000 and $1 million. The length of time the United States continued to support the FNLA is equally unclear, with estimates putting the cutoff date anywhere from 1969 to 1975. However, one thing is for certain: the United States funded the FNLA.

While American funding to the FNLA was supposed to be covert, the Portuguese knew what was going on, as is evident in a letter from Undersecretary George W. Ball in which he states he "cat-egorically assured Dr. Salazar that we were not providing assistance to Holden Roberto."[60] Obviously, if Ball had to assure Salazar, Salazar was suspicious.

The Politics of Containing Communism

The U.S. diplomatic and suspected economic support of the Angolans antagonized Portugal. Anti-American demonstrations broke out in Portugal's major cities, and Salazar expressed his extreme displeasure about U.S. actions at a NATO meeting in May 1961. While U.S. sympathies

UNITA soldiers receive weapons training at a camp near the Zambian border during the civil war in Angola.

may have lain with the anticolonial struggle, the battle to contain communism was a global one, and when the Portuguese became angry at U.S. diplomatic support of the Angolan rebels and threatened the U.S. military position in the Azores, the Kennedy administration was forced to rethink its approach.

In December 1962 the United States had to renegotiate its lease for military bases in the Azores, and Portuguese threats to refuse to renew the lease quickly put Kennedy's Angolan policies in check. The Americans, who had voted to condemn Portugal's violent repression of the Angolans a year before, now refused to do so again. The United States had clearly chosen its military interests in the fight to contain communism in Europe over those of the Angolan rebels.

However, U.S. officials also feared that communism would take root in Angola if they did nothing to stop it. As time went on, it became increasingly clear that the MPLA was being funded by the Soviet Union, and the U.S. government believed it needed to continue to fund the FNLA in order to retain its influence in Angola. The Kennedy administration's solution was to publicly present itself as squarely in Portugal's corner, while continuing to covertly fund the FNLA.

Double-Dealing

Some diplomats had difficulty with the covert nature of the funding given Holden Roberto in the early days. In the following excerpt from a March 17, 1964, memorandum sent to Secretary of State Dean Rusk by Undersecretary George W. Ball, Ball attacks the proposal to fund Roberto as "double-dealing," since the Portuguese had been assured that no such funding was taking place. The entire memorandum can be found at www.cphrc.org.uk.

> I wish to register an emphatic dissent to the proposal to provide [classified amount of support] to Holden Roberto . . . of the Angolan Provisional Government (GRAE).
>
> In filing this dissent, let me make it clear that I do not admire the methods or policies of the Portuguese Government in Angola. . . .
>
> *First, I object to this proposal as a destructive moral precedent for the American Government.*

The doling out of this money will constitute double-dealing on the part of the United States Government. You have on at least two occasions (in Lisbon and Athens in 1962) assured the Portuguese Foreign Minister that we engaged in no activities with Holden Roberto that we could not disclose to the Portuguese. You did tell the Foreign Minister that we had had for some time an intelligence arrangement for Holden Roberto. . . . Pursuant to my instructions, I categorically assured Dr. Salazar that we were not providing assistance to Holden Roberto—and, by implication, that we did not intend to do so.

To embark on a covert program of aid to Holden Roberto at this point would be a direct violation of confidence. I cannot believe that it is either good morals or good policy to put the United States Government in that position.

The End of a Regime Raises Hopes of Independence

Portuguese troops celebrate in the street following the 1974 overthrow of the Salazar regime.

In the end it was not the MPLA, the FNLA, or UNITA that ended colonialism in Angola. These groups fought for thirteen years with little or no results. Instead, it was the overthrow of the authoritarian Salazar regime in Portugal itself that brought about the demise of colonialism. This occurred on April 25, 1974, when military officers carried out a coup that toppled the regime and created a political group called the Movement of the Armed Forces (MFA) that assumed power.

Immediately following the overthrow, thoughts of independence ran high in Angola and for good reason. A man who appeared to be sympathetic to the anti-colonial cause, General Antonio de Spínola, was named president of the new Portuguese government in May 1974. Spínola held the influential post of Deputy Head of the Joint Chiefs of Staff of the Armed Forces when the Salazar regime had power in Portugal. However, he had been fired for openly challenging the government's policy of trying to solve problems in Angola through military force.

Spínola argued it was unrealistic to expect a military solution to the anticolonial wars "as long as the masses prove themselves willing to fight." He added that the Portuguese could never win the war because the Angolan people would always rise up and concluded that therefore "there remains only one way to end the conflict"[61] and that was by seeking out a political solution. With sympathetic friends in such high places, the anticolonial movements of Angola were optimistic about the future.

Spínola did not grant Angola—or any of Portugal's other African colonies—independence immediately. Instead, he suggested the colonies become states in the Portuguese united nation. In Spínola's view, the Portuguese settlers already in Angola would rule over the state as part of the Portuguese united nation while Angolan natives would be allowed to develop their own democracy and play

The Alvor Agreement

On January 15, 1975, representatives of the three liberation movements and the Portuguese government signed the Alvor Agreement, which was intended to facilitate the smooth transition of power from the Portuguese to the movements. The following is an excerpt from the Alvor Agreement that can be found at www.cphrc.org.uk.

Chapter 1 On the independence of Angola

Article 1

The Portuguese State recognizes the Liberation Movements—National Angolan Liberation Front (FNLA), the People's Movement for the Liberation of Angola (MPLA) and the National Union for Total Independence of Angola (UNITA)—as the sole legitimate representatives of the people of Angola.

Article 2

The Portuguese State solemnly restates its recognition of the right of the people of Angola to independence. . . .

Article 4

The independence and full sovereignty of Angola shall be solemnly proclaimed on 11 November 1975 in Angola by the President

of the Portuguese Republic or by a specially appointed representative of the President.

Article 5

Until independence is proclaimed, the power shall be wielded by the High Commissioner and by a Transitional Government, which shall take office on 31 January 1975.

Article 6

The Portuguese State and the three Liberation Movements formally affirm, under this agreement, a general ceasefire, already being observed de facto by their armed forces throughout Angolan territory.

After this date, any use of force other than as decided by the rightful authorities to prevent internal acts of violence or acts of aggression from outside the country shall be considered to be illicit. . . .

Article 8

The Portuguese State undertakes to transfer progressively, no later than the term of the transitional period, all the powers it enjoys and wields in Angola to the Angolan organs of sovereignty.

a role in the administration of the state. In other words, Spínola hoped to maintain control over Angola by giving its citizens more, but not total, power. Spínola's more conservative views on how to deal with the colonies were challenged by more radical segments of the MFA, which held a great deal of political power in Portugal and argued for complete and total independence of the colonies.

The Alvor Agreement

While Portuguese leaders debated the fate of the colonies, the anticolonial nationalist groups of Angola continued to fight against the Portuguese armed forces. After navigating the cease-fire process with each individual group, Spínola realized it would be politically impossible for his Portuguese united nation to come about and that full independence of the Portuguese colonies was inevitable. Unable to influence events in any other direction, on July 27, 1974, Spínola announced that the colonies would be granted full independence.

Although Spínola left office due to political pressure in late September, his successors continued to move towards Angolan independence. This eventually culminated in the Alvor Agreement named after the city in southern Portugal where it was signed. The agreement dictated how the transfer of power from Portugal to the three liberation movements was to be achieved. On January 15, 1975, the MPLA, FNLA, and UNITA move-

ments came together, recognized each other's right to be a part of the new government, and agreed to form a transitional government. Each of the three movements would select one person to be part of a presidential committee. In addition, other influential offices within the government would be split evenly between the movements and Portuguese representatives. The transitional government would rule Angola from January 31 until November 11, 1975, when the Portuguese would formally withdraw and turn over power to the Angolan president, who was to be elected no later than October 31.

The United States Versus the USSR in Angola

A showdown between the United States and the Soviet Union over Angola had been brewing since the early 1960s. Immediately following the coup, the United States had something akin to a hands-off policy. While they supported Spínola's Portuguese united nation idea, they did not interfere in Angola in any significant way. This decision was no doubt influenced by the fact that the USSR had stopped funding the MPLA in 1973 because Soviet advisers were apparently displeased with the state of the organization. Since the Soviets were not involved, U.S. fears of communism coming to power in Angola were allayed, and American officials saw very little need to be involved in the Angolan conflict.

However, the situation became more enticing when the three liberation groups and the Portuguese signed the Alvor Agreement. Both superpowers saw this as an opportunity to gain another ally in the world and resumed the funding of their respective Angolan rebel groups. Two weeks after the Alvor Agreement was signed, U.S. president Gerald Ford's administration approved three hundred thousand dollars to go to the FNLA. At the same time, the Soviets reinitiated aid to the MPLA, and, in conjunction with the Cubans, began airlifting weaponry and advisers to Angola. While the U.S. grant to the FNLA was nowhere near that which the MPLA received from the So-viets, it signaled to the people of the world—and to the Soviets in particular—that the United States was interested in wielding influence in Angola.

However, while the three groups had left each other alone to face the Portuguese, now that this common enemy was gone and power was up for grabs, hostilities arose between the MPLA and both the FNLA and UNITA. Since UNITA and the FNLA were opposed to the MPLA, the United States soon began to support UNITA as well. As foreign nations picked sides in the dispute, the Cold

Members of the Soviet-backed MPLA train at a military instruction center in Angola in 1974.

War Angolan teams began to firm up, with the USSR, the Soviet Bloc, and the Cubans supporting the MPLA, and the United States, Zaire, China, and South Africa supporting the FNLA and UNITA.

Operation Feature

Hearing that the Soviet Union had resumed funding the MPLA, the Ford administration was faced with a number of decisions about whether to increase U.S. funding to the FNLA and UNITA in Angola. In the wake of the devastating U.S. loss in Vietnam, President Ford's secretary of state, Henry Kissinger, was determined to stand up to the Soviets and counter their move in Africa. While the more extensive U.S. involvement in Angola was the result of many factors, it was due, in part, to Kissinger's insistence that the United States stand up to the Soviets to prove it still could.

As a result, the Ford administration decided to launch Operation Feature in July 1975. The operation was a covert program in which $32 million and $16 million in military supplies were funneled through Zaire to the FNLA. Suddenly, the United States found itself fully committed to an extensive covert action in Angola. This increased U.S. involvement, in turn, gave the Soviets greater freedom to escalate their efforts because it would now appear that they were countering U.S. efforts instead of trying to unfairly control Angola. In this way, the United States and the USSR became engaged in a struggle for influence in Angola. When one superpower increased its level of support, the other followed suit, and in the end both sides provided a great deal of financial and military support to the organization(s) they backed. Author John Prados details some of this support:

> The Americans acquired 2 Swift boats for the FNLA. . . . Eight assorted light planes were contracted, commandeered, or diverted. The Swift boats, 140 trucks, 300 radios, and 70 mortar sailed from Charlestown for Africa. . . .
>
> Soviet aid was estimated at $100 million by December 1975, and four times that amount by March. Weapons sent in early 1976 included T-54 tanks and MIG jet fighters.[62]

With the backing of the United States and Zaire as well as incredibly successful troops from South Africa, the FNLA and UNITA began to score military victories against the MPLA. Their goal was to reach the MPLA stronghold of Luanda, which was also the capital of Angola, before the Portuguese abdicated authority on November 11, 1975, so that they could declare themselves the government of Angola on independence day.

Portugal Exits the Scene

As the day of independence approached, the combined UNITA and FNLA forces were approaching Luanda rapidly. Roberto desperately wanted to be in the capital on independence day. Therefore, against the advice (and wishes) of his allies, Roberto launched an attack, sending troops to take Luanda. This was the beginning of the end for Roberto's forces. Facing an MPLA reinforced by Cuban troops and Soviet weapons, the anti-MPLA forces would not reach the goal of getting to Lu-

Funding to Angola

In December 1975 the Senate voted to stop all U.S. funding to Angolan nationalist forces fighting the MPLA. In a subsequent meeting of the National Security Council on December 22, President Ford expressed his dismay about this decision and his intentions to try to fight it. The report can be found at www.gwu.edu.

President Ford: Before we get into the basic part of the meeting, I want to take a minute to talk about Angola. The vote in the Senate on Angola was, to say the least, mildly deplorable. I cannot believe it represents a good policy for the U.S. and it is not fundamentally the way the American people think.

I made a short but tough statement on television, and I reiterated my position in an informal press conference. . . . I find [funding to FNLA and UNITA] the right thing to do. We should spend every dime legally that we decided upon. We should spend every nickel and do everything we can. Hopefully—and Secretary Kissinger recommended this option—it will lead to some kind of negotiated settlement.

If we become chicken because of the Senate vote, prospects will be bad. Every department should spend all it can legally—do all we can in that area.

anda by November 11, 1975. Instead, they were pushed back, and in the face of such superior and frightening weaponry, they eventually fled.

Thus the anti-MPLA forces did not take the capital, and on November 10, 1975, the Portuguese left and transferred power to all the people of Angola but to no one in particular. This left Angola without a government and in the throes of a civil war, which raged between rebel groups backed by the two superpowers.

Since the MPLA controlled the capital, they declared the People's Republic of Angola on November 11, 1975. The Soviet Union, the Soviet bloc countries, Cuba, and Brazil recognized this new state almost immediately. Outside the capital, the UNITA and FNLA forces declared their own government and continued to fight, but their government was not recognized by any other nation—not even the United States, which had funded the two groups.

Congress Discovers American Involvement

On December 13, 1975, *The New York Times* ran a front-page article exposing the U.S. government's covert operation in Angola. Fresh out of Vietnam and opposed to another lengthy and debilitating foreign entanglement, the reaction from Congress was swift. On December 19 Congress passed the first of two amendments—called the Clark Amendment—that halted all funding to anti-MPLA forces and prohibited further covert action.

South African soldiers carry a young Angolan refugee to a medical facility.

In a December 22 meeting of the National Security Council, President Ford called the vote "mildly deplorable" and responded with what he called a "tough statement" in favor of funding the movements. Determined not to "become chicken because of the Senate vote" and believing that funding these movements was "the right thing to do," Ford suggested, "Every department should spend all it can legally—do all we can in that area."[63]

Still, the United States had to withdraw most of its funding to the FNLA and the UNITA. With the Soviets continued funding of the MPLA, this significantly altered the situation in Angola. South Africa, in which the government sanctioned racial segregation, was now the principal supporter of these African nationalist movements. As a result of this unseemly alliance, many African nations chose to recognize the MPLA as the official government of Angola. On February 10 the Organization of African Unity officially recognized the People's Republic of Angola. In addition, Portugal recognized the MPLA's regime.

However, UNITA continued to wage a guerilla war against the MPLA regime. In 1981 the Reagan administration resumed aid to UNITA, and in 1985 the Clark Amendment was repealed, and the U.S. government openly assisted the organization. Then, in 1988, with all the forces reaching a stalemate and completely exhausted, it was the two superpowers that tried to put an end to the fighting. The United States, USSR, and Cuba came to an agreement to leave Angola. After many attempts at peace, fighting still continues in Angola today. However, all the outside backers have withdrawn their forces.

Chapter 8

Nicaragua and the Iran-Contra Affair

One of the final U.S. entanglements of the Cold War occurred in Nicaragua. The small Central American nation became an issue shortly after Ronald Reagan was elected president in 1980. In his opinion, communism was trying to take root in the United States's Central American backyard in the form of the Sandinistas, the regime that ruled Nicaragua. In the words of historian Nathan Miller, Reagan was convinced that "the Sandinistas and their allies in El Salvador planned to turn the area into another Cuba that the Soviets could use both as a base in the heart of the Americas and as a platform for subversion."[64]

Thus, the Reagan administration set out to fight the Sandinistas. This marked a shift in U.S. containment policy, a return to containment practiced by early Cold War presidents who committed the United States to stopping communism wherever it arose. However, Reagan's containment policy differed slightly from that of Kennedy. The Sandinista regime in Nicaragua was an already existing Communist nation, and, unlike the FNLA or UNITA in Angola, the country of Nicaragua was by no means up for grabs. While Reagan argued he was containing communism by attempting to keep Sandinista influence from spreading, he was also trying to "roll it back" by attacking—however covertly—a Communist nation in the hopes it would "fall" to anti-Communist forces.

A New Regime Takes Power and a New President Takes Office

The United States has a long history of involvement in Nicaraguan affairs. It began in the early twentieth century and includes the deployment of the marines to Nicaragua on a number of occasions under the auspices of stabilizing the area. In 1978 the U.S.-backed Somoza regime fell from power when the assassination of opposition leader Pedro Joaquin Chamorro led to uprisings against the Somoza government. It was at this time that a nationalist group calling themselves the Frente Sandinista de Liberación (FSLN), or the Sandinistas, came to power.

After taking power, the Sandinistas set out to complete the revolution they had begun, all the while trying to be aware of the pitfalls they had to avoid. Knowing how difficult the United States would make matters for Nicaragua if the Sandinistas expressed socialist beliefs, they attempted to present a milder form of socialism to their northern neighbors. The Sandinistas did nationalize some lands but only those of the Somozas and their associates. The Sandinistas also began some of the most noteworthy social reforms in recent history. However, Rea-

gan saw the Sandinistas as a Communist government taking its lead from Moscow and did everything in his power to stop the Sandinistas from achieving their foreign policy objectives.

Reagan's diagnosis of the Sandinista regime as a Soviet pawn was the result of a number of factors. In conjunction with the Sandinistas' nationalization of some Nicaraguan lands, the FSLN had established ties with a number of nations, including Castro's Cuba and the Soviet bloc. In addition, Nicaragua was—along with these other nations—providing arms to guerilla warriors in El Salvador. Newly elected president Reagan saw this as a

Sandinista guerillas wielding slingshots and machine guns take cover during the 1978 coup.

Looters plunder a market during a 1978 riot in Esteli, Nicaragua.

significant Soviet threat in which the Soviets would take control of Central America and use it as a springboard to carry out operations against the United States. By March 1981 he signed a Presidential Finding that approved the development of an operation to stop the flow of arms to El Salvador. Reagan believed communism was trying to gain a foothold in Central America, and he resolved to stop it. The result was the largest U.S. covert operation since Vietnam.

The Reagan Doctrine

The Reagan administration's intervention in Nicaragua marked a new chapter in the history of the U.S. containment of communism during the Cold War. Since the end of the Vietnam War, U.S. presidents had had a more limited view of containment, set forth in the Nixon Doctrine. In contrast, Reagan returned to stopping communism anywhere. In addition, he took this one step further and applied offensive force against communism. No Communist regime was attacking Nicaragua, and the country was not without a government. The administration simply defined the Sandinistas as

Communists and wanted to replace them with an anti-Communist regime.

This dedication to supporting "freedom fighters" in an attempt to deal communism a loss came to be known as the Reagan Doctrine. Reagan announced it as part of his 1985 State of the Union Address. It confirmed the willingness of the United States to assist "those who are risking their lives—on every continent, from Afghanistan to Nicaragua—to defy Soviet-supported aggression and secure

The Reagan Doctrine

In his 1985 State of the Union Address, President Ronald Reagan put forth what came to be called the "Reagan Doctrine," a commitment not just to containing communism everywhere, but to rolling it back. The following is an excerpt from that speech. The speech can be found at www.thegipper.com.

> And tonight, we declare anew to our fellow citizens of the world: Freedom is not the sole prerogative of a chosen few; it is the universal right of all God's children. Look to where peace and prosperity flourish today.

It is in homes that freedom built. Victories against poverty are greatest and peace most secure where people live by laws that ensure free press, free speech, and freedom to worship, vote, and create wealth.

Our mission is to nourish and defend freedom and democracy, and to communicate these ideals everywhere we can. . . .

We must stand by all our democratic allies. And we must not break faith with those who are risking their lives—on every continent, from Afghanistan to Nicaragua—to defy Soviet-supported aggression and secure rights which have been ours from birth.

The Sandinista dictatorship of Nicaragua, with full Cuban-Soviet bloc support, not only persecutes its people, the church, and denies a free press, but arms and provides bases for Communist terrorists attacking neighboring states. Support for freedom fighters is self-defense and totally consistent with the OAS and U.N. Charters. It is essential that the Congress continue all facets of our assistance to Central America. I want to work with you to support the democratic forces whose struggle is tied to our own security.

President Reagan supported rolling back communism around the world in 1985.

rights which have been ours from birth."
And, he argued, "Support for freedom
fighters is self-defense"[65] for the United
States.

Supporting "Freedom Fighters"

In line with his commitment to roll back
communism in Nicaragua, in the fall of
1981 Reagan approved CIA director
William Casey's detailed plan for an operation in Nicaragua. It called for roughly
five hundred Nicaraguan rebels to be
trained as a secret force that would sabotage targets and try to encourage unrest
in Nicaragua. Believing Congress might
fear the advent of another Vietnam if CIA
advisers handled the training of these
rebel forces, Argentine and Honduran

military forces would do the training
while the United States paid for it. (When
the Argentines dropped out of the project in 1982, the CIA did in fact train the
rebels.) The budget for the entire special
operation was $19 million.

Reagan threw U.S. support behind a
rebel group calling themselves the Contras, a small group of anti-Sandinista
guerillas with a base in Honduras. The
CIA augmented the already existing contra forces with an assortment of men who
could train and advise them. Many of
these old CIA contacts had provided assistance in Vietnam, and in combination

*U.S.-backed contra forces conduct training
exercises at a camp in Honduras.*

PsyOps Manual

The CIA's Psychological Operations (PsyOps) in Guerilla Warfare Manual was designed to train the contras. However, it came under fire for many of the tactics it promoted such as hiring professional criminals to do "jobs" and creating situations that would result in the shooting of civilians. Below is a portion of the manual that caused a great deal of concern in the United States when it was discovered. The manual can be found in its entirety at www.webcom.com.

> Our cadres will be mobilized in the largest number possible, together with persons who have been affected by the Communist dictatorship, whether their possessions have been stolen from them, they have been incarcerated, or tortured, or suffered from any other type of aggression against them. They will be mobilized toward the areas where the hostile and criminal elements of the FSLN, CDS and others live, with an effort for them to be armed with clubs, iron rods, placards and if possible, small firearms, which they will carry hidden.
>
> If possible, professional criminals will be hired to carry out specific selected "jobs. . . ."
>
> Specific tasks will be assigned to others, in order to create a "martyr" for the cause, taking the demonstrators to a confrontation with the authorities, in order to bring about uprisings or shootings, which will cause the death of one or more persons, who would become the martyrs, a situation that should be made use of immediately against the regime, in order to create greater conflicts.

with the contras and other ex–Somoza guardsmen, they were soon a well-trained, functioning counterrevolutionary force of twenty thousand men that was well supplied with state-of-the-art military equipment.

The first real strikes against the Sandinistas occurred in mid-March 1982 when the contras blew up two bridges to disrupt transportation in Nicaragua and inspire fear in its civilians. While sabotage efforts such as this continued on the military front, the Americans also attacked on the economic front by working to deny international loans to Nicaragua. However, despite the fact that there was internal unrest in the FSLN and they were better armed, the contras accom-

plished very little in 1982. Still, their funding was increased for the following year to $21 million. They would receive $24 million the following year.

Accounts of the behavior of these forces were filled with charges of human rights abuses, internal bickering, and drug smuggling. Not only do the contras seem to have behaved deplorably but they also failed to achieve any significant gains, even after several years of CIA funding. In late 1983 the CIA took matters into its own hands. Casey attempted to double his forces, and in an attempt to isolate the Sandinistas, the CIA began to mine the Nicaraguan ports (in violation of international law) in a way that would appear as though the rebel forces were responsible when the Nicaraguans figured it out, which they did on January 3, 1984.

An Angry Congress

In 1984, despite U.S. attempts to discredit the first Nicaragua post-coup elections, Daniel Ortega Saavedra, the leader of the FSLN, was elected president of Nicaragua. Ortega was openly Marxist and anti-American, and his position as president deepened some Americans' fears of a Communist takeover of Central America. As a result, the battle with the contras intensified. At the same time, rumors of the CIA's breach of international law by mining the ports came to light, as did the existence of training manuals published by the CIA that encouraged the assassination of Nicaraguan citizens as a means to create unrest. As a result of these disclosures, members of Congress became increasingly leery of the Nicaragua venture.

By October, Congress was angry and ready to take action against the secret war in Nicaragua, which continually proved to be less than secret. Members of Congress began to notice huge discrepancies between the actual events in Nicaragua and those being reported in the briefings Congress received. Some members also found the cost of the venture daunting. As a result, Congress approved the first of a series of laws that would eventually culminate in the Boland Amendment, which stated that the U.S. government could provide only humanitarian, or "non-lethal," aid to the contras. That is, the U.S. government could not *legally* provide the contras with military supplies or the means to procure them.

Phase Two Begins

However, when it came to the not-so-secret war against the Sandinistas, President Reagan would not be stopped. "Anyone who thought these restrictions would force President Reagan to reduce or close down the secret war," historian Nathan Miller writes, "obviously had not reckoned with the depth of his commitment to the Nicaraguan rebels."[66]

When Congress prohibited funding, Reagan worked hard to keep the cash flowing to his freedom fighters. He lobbied Congress to give the contras a significant amount of *humanitarian aid,* money and supplies that cannot be used for military purposes. Then, Reagan's White House asked private citizens/groups for aid for the contra cause. Reagan also pursued indirect funding of the contras by urging and coercing America's allies to give to the Nicaraguan rebels. As the authors of *The Iran-Contra Connection* point out, "In July 1985 the Reagan Administration not only got $27 million 'non-lethal' aid out of Congress for the contras, it also figured out a way to 'legalize' shaking down U.S. aid recipients for contributions to the mercenaries."[67]

Caught

As Reagan tried to woo Congress and the American public into funding the con-

Former Security Advisor Robert C. McFarlane (left) faces a joint House-Senate Committee during the 1987 hearings which exposed the Iran-Contra affair.

tras, a more clandestine method of providing funds for the contras developed. Reagan wanted more money, and he knew he could not get it from Congress. Yet, the Reagan administration did manage to provide money for military aid to the contras without congressional approval. It was able to do so by exchanging arms for hostages and money from Iran—a country Reagan had vowed never to do business with and had referred to as "Murder, Inc." The money received in the transaction was then diverted to the contras. Reagan had managed to procure up-

ward of $30 million dollars for the Nicaraguan freedom fighters in this manner.

However, the administration did not successfully cover its tracks. In 1986 a magazine in Beirut, Lebanon, divulged the fact that Robert McFarlane (who had left the National Security Council a year earlier) secretly visited Tehran in May 1986, at which time the United States and the

Iranians reached a deal to swap arms for hostages. President Reagan had repeatedly said he would never negotiate with terrorists, but now he was said to have authorized the mission to do just that. Reagan categorically denied the incident, but a few days after the article appeared in Beirut, Attorney General Edwin Meese confirmed the reports. The public scandal that resulted came to be called the Iran-Contra Affair.

The Iran-Contra Affair

The core issue of the Iran-Contra Affair was remarkably simple: it appeared the president had broken the law by sanctioning military aid to the contras after Congress prohibited it. However, the affair itself and the number of players involved were so complex that exactly what happened may never be known. After Meese confirmed the arms-for-hostages swap (which Reagan later acknowledged), Lawrence E. Walsh was chosen to act as an independent special prosecutor and investigate both the arms sale and the diversion of funds.

President Reagan also wanted his own investigation and created a review board headed by former Republican senator

Summary of the Report of the Independent Counsel

Following its investigation of the Iran-Contra Affair, the Independent Counsel came to the following "overall conclusions." The report summary can be found at www.webcom.com.

The investigations and prosecutions have shown that high-ranking Administration officials violated laws and executive orders in the Iran/contra matter.

Independent Counsel concluded that:

the sales of arms to Iran contravened United States Government policy and may have violated the Arms Export Control Act. . .

the policies behind both the Iran and contra operations were fully reviewed and developed at the highest levels of the Reagan Administration . . .

the Iran operations were carried out with the knowledge of, among others, President Ronald Reagan, Vice President George Bush, Secretary of State George P. Shultz, Secretary of Defense Caspar W. Weinberger, Director of Central Intelligence William J. Casey, and national security advisers Robert C. McFarlane and John M. Poindexter; of these officials, only Weinberger and Shultz dissented from the policy decision, and Weinberger eventually acquiesced by ordering the Department of Defense to provide the necessary arms;

and large volumes of highly relevant, contemporaneously created documents were systematically and willfully withheld from investigators by several Reagan Administration officials.

following the revelation of these operations in October and November 1986, Reagan Administration officials deliberately deceived the Congress and the public about the level and extent of official knowledge of and support for these operations.

John Tower to evaluate the situation. Washington became ensconced in scandal, and over the next eight months the American public watched televised hearings on the matter in which the underhanded dealings of the operation were revealed to the nation and the world.

The official reports on the Iran-Contra Affair were made public, and the Tower Commission was kind to the president. It criticized him for his lack of oversight and poor management of the people below him. In response, Reagan accepted responsibility for actions of the people under his command. The Independent Counsel's Report was not quite so generous. It concluded that the sale of arms to Iran was both against U.S. policy and possibly a violation of the Arms Export Control Act. As for funding contras, the Independent Counsel found it to be in direct violation of the Boland Amendment. Walsh concluded, "the policies behind both the Iran and contra operations were fully reviewed and developed at the highest levels of the Reagan Administration."[68] This implicated the president in the affair to a much greater degree than had the Tower Commission.

Thus, Reagan's deep commitment to containing communism had been a guiding force in his presidency. It led to his willingness to entangle the United States in the affairs of Nicaragua in an attempt to try to overthrow the existing Sandinista government. It also led to his bending—and some would argue breaking—of U.S. laws to continue to fund the contras once Congress had abandoned the containment issue in Nicaragua, which resulted in the Iran-Contra affair.

Containment in the Post Cold War World

By the time the prosecutions in the Iran-Contra Affair wrapped up in 1992, the Cold War was officially over. Mikhail Gorbachev's attempts to reform the Soviet system had led to its downfall. The Berlin Wall came down, the Soviet satellites and Baltic States had declared their independence, and the United States could declare itself—and its way of life—the winner.

Throughout the Cold War, the United States had boasted incredible victories and tried to recover from embarrassing defeats as it became increasingly involved in the affairs of other nations around the world. A country whose first president had warned strenuously against entangling alliances had seen its power buoyed by intervention in external situations. It had also suffered the embarrassment of the Bay of Pigs debacle and the heartbreak of the Vietnam War as a result.

Immediately following the demise of the Soviet Union, it was difficult for the people of the world to imagine a global atmosphere free of the tension between two nuclear superpowers, which had dominated international politics for so long. Throughout the Cold War, the U.S. policy of containment of communism had brought it into constant conflict with the Soviet Union and had caused a long line of presidents to commit American resources and troops to stopping the spread of communism. In the process, the concept of containment had grown and changed—so much so that nearly every president had his own "doctrine" that advanced the policy. Suddenly, in the absence of a strong Soviet Union, there was no other nation bent on world domination and no communism to contain.

The struggle between the superpowers had shaped world history for nearly half a century. Once the struggle ended, some problems were immediately resolved. For instance, some of the conflicts and civil wars in emerging nations

such as Nicaragua simply faded away without the superpowers to support and encourage them. However, at the same time world affairs became less predictable. After the breakup of the Soviet Union at Cold War's end, the world saw the revival of age-old ethnic conflicts in parts of the former Soviet bloc that led to frightening incidents of ethnic persecution and cleansing. In the absence of the superpowers, the world also saw the rise of a more substantial terrorist effort against the United States and the American fight to contain that threat, a threat that is not as easy to identify or fight as communism.

★ Chronology of Events ★

1945

February 4–11: President Roosevelt, British prime minister Churchill, and Soviet premier Stalin meet at Yalta in the Ukraine to discuss how to administer postwar Europe. They divide Germany into four occupation zones and Berlin into four corresponding zones.

September: Ho Chi Minh declares Vietnam's independence. Soon after, the British grant the French authority in Vietnam.

1946

February 22: George F. Kennan sends his "long telegram" explaining the Soviet threat to Washington.

March 5: Winston Churchill makes his "Iron Curtain" speech.

June 5: The Marshall Plan is announced.

July: Kennan, writing under the anonymous name of "X," publishes an article in *Foreign Affairs* that introduces containment theory to the world.

1948

June: The Soviet Berlin Blockade begins, as does the American response, the Berlin Airlift.

1950

April: National Security Council document no. 68 (NSC-68) is issued, and a sig-nificant U.S. military buildup follows as a result of its recommendations.

June 25: North Korea invades South Korea, and President Truman commits American troops to the war.

July 26: The U.S. government approves $15 million in military aid to the French for the war in Indochina (the southeast Asian peninsula).

1951

July: Cease-fire talks between North and South Korea begin, but disagreements over how to handle prisoners of war make peace impossible.

1952

The Free Officers led by Gamal Abdel Nasser and General Muhammad Naguib overthrow King Farouk in Egypt and seize power.

1953

July 27: Armistice agreement between North and South Korea is signed.

1954

May 7: The French surrender to Ho Chi Minh's forces at Dien Bien Phu, Vietnam.

July: The Geneva Accords are agreed upon. The accords call for a cessation of hostilities and divide Vietnam at the seventeenth parallel pending a nationwide election in two year's time.

July 27: The United States brokers a deal between Great Britain and Nasser's administration that ends British occupation of the Suez Canal.

1955

January: The United States begins to directly fund and train the South Vietnamese military.

July 16: With United States approval, South Vietnamese leader Ngo Dinh Diem refuses to hold elections that would most likely have reunited Vietnam under Ho Chi Minh.

1956

July 19: The United States cancels funding to Egypt for the Aswan Dam.

October 29: Britain, France, and Israel attack Egypt in an attempt to reclaim the Suez Canal.

1958

March 9: Eisenhower Doctrine is announced.

1959

January 1: Fidel Castro comes to power in Cuba.

1961

April 17: The United States–backed attempt to overthrow Castro at the Bay of Pigs fails.

August 13: The Berlin Wall is erected.

October: Maxwell Taylor and Walt Whitman Rostow visit Vietnam and return with recommendations that the president give the South Vietnamese government more financial and military aid.

1962

October: The Cuban Missile Crisis occurs.

1963

November 22: President Kennedy is assassinated, and Lyndon B. Johnson becomes president of the United States.

1964

August: North Vietnamese torpedo boats launch two attacks on the U.S. destroyer, the *Maddox*, in the Gulf of Tonkin. This leads Congress to pass the Gulf of Tonkin Resolution, which grants the president extraordinary power to wage the war in Vietnam.

1966

December: United States personnel in Vietnam totals four hundred thousand.

1967

United States personnel in Vietnam increases to five hundred thousand, and antiwar protests rise in the United States.

1968

March 31: President Johnson announces that he is suspending the bombing of North Vietnam and initiating peace talks in hopes of ending American involvement in Vietnam. He also announces he will not run for reelection.

1969

January 1: Richard M. Nixon takes office as the president of the United States.

July 25: The Nixon Doctrine is announced. It states that the Americans will no longer automatically fight communism in Asia (or elsewhere in the world). Instead, they will do so only under certain circumstances.

December: American troop strength in Vietnam is decreased by sixty thousand.

1973

January: A peace treaty is signed between the United States and Vietnam.

1974

April 25: A coup topples the Salazar regime in Portugal.

July 27: President Spínola announces that Portuguese colonies will be granted full independence.

1975

January 15: The Angolan anticolonial movements, the MPLA, FNLA, and UNITA movements, come together and sign the Alvor Agreement, which outlines a plan for the transfer of power in the former colony. Soon after, the United States and the USSR reinitiate funding to the FNLA and MPLA respectively.

April: South Vietnam falls to the Communist North.

December 13: A *New York Times* article reveals the secret funding of the FNLA and UNITA. Congress reacts by passing the Clark Amendment and forbidding any further support to the Angolan rebel groups.

1976

February 10: The Organization of African Unity officially recognizes the People's Republic of Angola as does Portugal.

1978

The Sandinistas come to power in Nicaragua.

1981

January: Ronald Reagan takes office as the president of the United States.

March: CIA training of the contras begins in Honduras.

1982

March: The contras make their first real strikes against the Sandinistas when they blow up two bridges in Nicaragua.

1984

October: Congress approves the first of a series of laws that state that the U.S. government can provide only humanitarian, or "non lethal," aid to the contras.

1985

February: In his State of the Union Address, Reagan announces the Reagan Doctrine, which calls on the United States to support "freedom fighters," such as the contras in Nicaragua.

1986

May: Robert McFarlane secretly visits Teheran to arrange a deal with the Iranians to swap arms for hostages.

November 3: A magazine in Beirut, Lebanon, divulges the fact that McFarlane arranged such a deal, and Reagan denies it.

1987

February: The Tower Commission releases its report on the Iran-Contra Affair.

Shortly thereafter, the Independent Counsel's report on the incident is released.

1989

November 9: The Berlin Wall falls.

☆ Notes ☆

Introduction: Washington's Warnings

1. Quoted in P.M.H. Bell, *The World Since 1945: An International History.* New York: Oxford University Press, 2001, p. 55.
2. Quoted in Bell, *The World Since 1945,* p. 55.
3. Quoted in Bell, *The World Since 1945,* p. 55.

Chapter 1: Containing Communism

4. George F. Kennan, Excerpts from Telegraphic Message from Moscow, February 22, 1946, *Vincent Ferraro's Home Page.* www.mtholyoke.edu.
5. Kennan, Excerpts from Telegraphic Message from Moscow.
6. Winston Churchill, "Sinews of Peace" Speech, March 5, 1946, *Churchill Center.* www.winstonchurchill.org.
7. Churchill, "Sinews of Peace" Speech.
8. Dwight D. Eisenhower, Presidential Press Conference, April 7, 1954, *Professor James M. Lindsay's Home Page.* www.uiowa.edu.
9. Quoted in Bell, *The World Since 1945,* p. 78.
10. Harry S. Truman, Address Before a Joint Session of Congress, March 12, 1947, *Fletcher School of Law and Diplo-*

macy. www.tufts.edu.
11. Truman, Address Before a Joint Session of Congress.
12. Quoted in Walter LaFeber, *America, Russia, and the Cold War, 1945–1990.* New York: McGraw-Hill, 1991, p. 49.
13. George Marshall, Harvard University Address, June 5, 1947, *Radio Free Europe.* www.rferl.org.
14. X (George F. Kennan), "The Sources of Soviet Conduct," *Foreign Affairs,* July 1947. darkwing.uoregon.edu.
15. X (George F. Kennan), "The Sources of Soviet Conduct."

Chapter 2: Berlin

16. Alexander S. Payushkin, Letter to the U.S. Secretary of State, July 14, 1948, *Truman Presidential Museum & Library.* www.trumanlibrary.org.
17. Quoted in *Public Broadcasting System,* "People & Events: The Berlin Blockade." www.pbs.org.
18. James Forrestal, *The Forrestal Diaries,* ed. Walter Millis. New York: Viking Press, 1951, p. 454.
19. Quoted in D.M. Giangreco and Robert E. Griffin, *Airbridge to Berlin— The Berlin Crisis of 1948, Its Origins and Aftermath.* 1988, Novato, CA: Presidio,

as it appears at www.trumanlibrary.org. www.trumanlibrary.org.

20. Quoted in Bell, *The World Since 1945*, p. 133.

21. Record of meeting between N.S. Khrushchev and W. Ulbricht. *CNN*. www.cnn.com.

22. Arthur Schlesinger Jr., "Reform and Revolt," in John M. Blum, William S. McFeely, Edmund S. Morgan, Arthur Schlesinger Jr., Kenneth Stampp, and C. Vann Woodward, *The National Experience: A History of the United States*, 7th ed. San Diego: Harcourt Brace Jovanovich, 1980, p. 750.

23. John F. Kennedy, Broadcast to the American Public: July 25, 1961, *CNN*. www.cnn.com.

Chapter 3: Korea: Containing Communism in Asia

24. National Security Council, Paper no. 68 (NSC-68), *Federation of American Scientists*. www.fas.org.

25. LaFeber, *America, Russia, and the Cold War, 1945–1990*, p. 99.

26. Bell, *The World Since 1945*, p. 107.

27. Eben A. Ayers, "Resolution Concerning the Complaint of Aggression Upon the Republic of Korea Adopted at the 474th Meeting of the Security Council," June 27, 1950, in papers of Eben A. Ayers, *Truman Presidential Museum & Library*. www.trumanlibrary.org.

28. George M. Elsey, Summary of June 25, 1950, Blair House meeting, in papers of George M. Elsey, *Truman Presidential Museum & Library*. www.trumanlibrary.org.

29. LaFeber, *America, Russia, and the Cold War, 1945–1990*, p. 114.

30. Nathan Miller, *Spying for America: The Hidden History of U.S. Intelligence*. New York: Marlowe & Company, 1997, p. 321.

Chapter 4: Egypt: Arab Nationalism Versus Containment

31. Adeed Dawisha, "Egypt," in Yezid Sayigh and Avi Shlaim, eds., *The Cold War and the Middle East*. New York: Oxford University Press, 1997, p. 27.

32. Quoted in LeFabre, *America, Russia, and the Cold War, 1945–1990*, p. 155.

33. Felix Gilbert with David Clay Large, *The End of the European Era, 1890 to the Present*. New York: W.W. Norton, 1991, p. 415.

34. Ray Takeyh, *The Origins of the Eisenhower Doctrine: The US, Britain and Nasser's Egypt 1953–1957*. New York: St. Martin's Press, 2000, p. 139.

35. Dwight D. Eisenhower, "Special Message to the Congress on the situation in the Middle East," January 5, 1957, *Dwight D. Eisenhower Library at the University of Texas*. www.eisenhower.utexas.edu.

Chapter 5: Cuba

36. LaFeber, *America, Russia, and the Cold War*, p. 208.

37. Bell, *The World Since 1945*, p. 138.

38. McGeorge Bundy, Memorandum from the President's Special Assistant for National Security Affairs to President Kennedy, April 18, 1961, *U.S. Department of State*, vol. 10, document no. 119. www.state.gov.

39. Arthur Schlesinger Jr., Memorandum from the President's Special Assistant to President Kennedy, May 3, 1961, *U.S. Department of State*, vol. 10, document no. 196. www.state.gov.

40. Schlesinger, Memorandum from the President's Special Assistant to President Kennedy.

41. Edward Lansdale, "Program Review [The Cuba Project]," February 20, 1962, *Parascope.com*. www.parascope.com.

42. John F. Kennedy, Speech Announcing the Quarantine Against Cuba, October 22, 1962, *Vincent Ferraro's Home Page*. www.mtholyoke.edu.

43. John F. Kennedy, Speech Announcing the Quarantine Against Cuba.

44. John F. Kennedy, Speech Announcing the Quarantine Against Cuba.

45. John F. Kennedy, Letter to Chairman Nikita Khrushchev, October 22, 1962, *U.S. Department of State*, vol. 11, document no. 44. www.state.gov.

46. *U.S. Department of State*, vol. 11, document no. 48, Telegram from the U.S. Embassy in the Soviet Union, October 23, 1962. www.state.gov.

47. *U.S. Department of State*, Telegram to the U.S. Embassy in the Soviet Union, vol. 11, document no. 52, October 23, 1962. www.state.gov.

48. Richard Reeves, "13 Days in October," *New York Times*, October 8, 1997. www.mtholyoke.edu.

Chapter 6: Vietnam

49. U.S. Senate Committee on Foreign Relations, 90th Congress, 1st Session, *Vincent Ferraro's Home Page*. www.mtholyoke.edu.

50. Dwight D. Eisenhower, *Mandate for Change, 1953–56*. Garden City, NY: Doubleday, 1963, p. 372.

51. Robert F. Kennedy in third oral history interview with John Barlow Martin, April 30, 1964, *Kennedy Assassination Homepage*. http://mcadams.posc.mu.edu.

52. Quoted in Stanley Karnow, *Vietnam: A History*. New York: Penguin Books, 1997, p. 265.

53. LaFeber, *America, Russia, and the Cold War, 1945–1990*, pp. 230–31.

54. Quoted in LaFeber, *America, Russia, and the Cold War, 1945–1990*, p. 238.

55. *HBC News*, Joint Resolution of Congress, August 7, 1974. www.luminet.net.

56. Miller, *Spying for America*, p. 382.

57. LaFeber, *America, Russia, and the Cold War, 1945–1990*, p. 259.

58. Richard Nixon, Speech on November 3, 1969, *Temple University OnLine Learning Program*. http://oll.temple.edu.

Chapter 7: Angola

59. Fernando Andresen Guimarães, *The Origins of the Angolan Civil War: Foreign Intervention and Domestic Political Con-

flict. New York: St. Martin's Press, 1998, p. 179.

60. George W. Ball, Memorandum sent to Secretary of State Dean Rusk, March 17, 1964, *cphrc portugal's history on-line*. www.cphrc.org.uk.

61. Quoted in Guimaràes, *The Origins of the Angolan Civil War*, p. 86.

62. John Prados, *President's Secret Wars: CIA and Pentagon Covert Operations Since World War II*. New York: William Morrow, 1986, p. 342–43.

63. Meeting of the National Security Council, December 22, 1975, *George Washington University*. www.gwu.edu.

Chapter 8: Nicaragua and the Iran-Contra Affair

64. Miller, *Spying for America*, p. 427.

65. Ronald Reagan, 1985 State of the Union Address, *The Gipper.com*. www.thegipper.com.

66. Miller, *Spying for America*, p. 430.

67. Jonathan Marshall, Peter Dale Scott, and Jane Hunter, *The Iran-Contra Connection: Secret Teams and Covert Operations in the Reagan Era*. Boston: South End Press, 1987, p. 111.

68. Summary of the Report of the Independent Counsel, *Pink Noise Studios*. www.webcom.com.

★ For Further Reading ★

Books

Jonathan Neale, *The American War: Vietnam 1960–1975*. Chicago: Bookmarks, 2001. This is a straightforward attempt to tell the story of Vietnam from the Vietnamese perspective in an accessible writing style.

Himilce Novas, *Everything You Need to Know about Latino History*. New York: Plume, 1994. This is a great book for the basic facts of Latino history presented in a question and answer format.

Katherine Sibley, *The Cold War*. Westport, CT: Greenwood Press, 1998. This is a good introduction to the basic events of the Cold War.

Websites

CNN's Cold War Website (www.cnn.com). This may very well be the most comprehensive Cold War site on the Web. It features episode recaps from CNN's Cold War series. There is also an option for full transcripts. It has interviews with a number of people on each topic as well as important primary documents.

PBS (www.pbs.org). This is Public Broadcasting System's Website, which contains a very useful Cold War section called "The Race for the Superbomb." The site also has an archive of great American speeches.

Pink Noise Studios (www.webcom.com). Contains a number of documents on U.S. covert operations during the Cold War.

Truman Presidential Museum & Library (www.trumanlibrary.org). This is by far one of the most comprehensive early Cold War sites on the Web. It now hosts the Project WhistleStop content, which amounts to hundreds of primary documents on early Cold War events such as the Truman Doctrine, the Marshall Plan, the Korean War, and the State of Israel.

⋆ **Works Consulted** ⋆

Books

P.M.H. Bell, *The World Since 1945: An International History*. New York: Oxford University Press, 2001. This is an excellent, comprehensive overview of the Cold War.

Adead Dawisha, "Egypt," in Yezid Sayigh and Avi Shlaim, eds., *The Cold War and the Middle East*. New York: Oxford Univiersity Press, 1997. A collection of essays on the various countries that make up the Middle East.

Dwight D. Eisenhower, *Mandate for Change, 1953–56*. Garden City, NY: Doubleday, 1963. Eisenhower's biography contains a great deal of information on his Cold War policies.

James Forrestal, *The Forrestal Diaries*. Ed. Walter Millis. New York: Viking Press, 1951. The diaries of President Truman's secretary of defense, James Forrestal.

Felix Gilbert with David Clay Large, *The End of the European Era, 1890 to the Present*. New York: W.W. Norton, 1991. This is a good overview of European history in the twentieth century.

Fernando Andresen Guimarães, *The Origins of the Angolan Civil War: Foreign Intervention and Domestic Political Conflict.* New York: St. Martin's Press, 1998. This is an excellent academic text on the Angolan Revolution, the liberation movements, and the foreign nations that provided outside assistance to them.

Stanley Karnow, *Vietnam: A History*. New York: Penguin Books, 1997. An in-depth history of the Vietnam War written by Pulitzer Prize–winning journalist, Stanley Karnow.

Walter LaFeber, *America, Russia, and the Cold War, 1945–1990*. New York: Mc-Graw-Hill, 1991. LaFeber's accessible writing makes this by far the best Cold War overview.

Jonathan Marshall, Peter Dale Scott, and Jane Hunter, *The Iran-Contra Connection: Secret Teams and Covert Operations in the Reagan Era*. Boston: South End, 1987. This is a fairly thorough account of the Iran-Contra Affair, the players, and the confusing events that made it the spectacle it was.

Nathan Miller, *Spying for America: The Hidden History of U.S. Intelligence*. New York: Marlowe, 1997. Miller relates the history of United States intelligence from the Revolutionary War to the mid-nineties.

John Prados, *Presidents' Secret Wars: CIA and Pentagon Covert Operations Since*

World War II. New York: William Morrow, 1986. Prados does a good job of explaining all the little details of the covert operations during the Cold War.

Arthur Schlesinger Jr., "Reform and Revolt," in John M. Blum, William S. McFeely, Edmund S. Morgan, Arthur Schlesinger Jr., Kenneth Stampp, and C. Vann Woodward, *The National Experience: A History of the United States*. 7th Ed. San Diego: Harcourt Brace Jovanovich, 1989. A great overview of American history.

Ray Takeyh, *The Origins of the Eisenhower Doctrine: The US, Britain, and Nasser's Egypt 1953–1957*. New York: St. Martin's Press, 2000. This is an in-depth and extremely complex look at United States foreign policy towards Egypt.

Thomas W. Walker and Ariel C. Armony, eds., *Repression, Resistance, and Democratic Transition in Central America*. Wilmington, DE: Scholarly Resources Books, 2000. This book discusses many of the tactics employed by Central American nations to procure independence. It includes chapters on Nicaragua.

Internet Sources

Eban A. Ayers, "Resolution Concerning the Complaint of Agression upon the Republic of Korea Adopted at the 474th Meeting of the Security Council, June 27, 1950," in papers of Eban A. Ayers, *Truman Presidential Museum & Library*. www.trumanlibrary.org.

George W. Ball, Memorandum to Secretary of State Dean Rusk, March 17, 1964, *cphrc portugal's history on-line*. www.cphrc.org.uk.

McGeorge Bundy, Memorandum from the President's Special Assistant for National Security Affairs to President Kennedy, April 18, 1961, *U.S. Department of State*, Vol. 10, Document no. 119. www.state.gov.

Winston Churchill, "Sinews of Peace" Speech, March 5, 1946, *Churchill Center*. www.winstonchurchill.org.

CNN, Record of meeting between N.S. Khrushchev and W. Ulbricht. www.cnn.com.

Dwight D. Eisenhower, Presidential Press Conference, April 7, 1954, *Professor James M. Lindsay's Home Page*. www.uiowa.edu.

———, "Special Message to the Congress on the Situation in the Middle East," January 5, 1957, *Dwight D. Eisenhower Library at the University of Texas*. www.eisenhower.utexas.edu.

George M. Elsey, Summary of June 25, 1950, Blair House meeting, in papers of George M. Elsey, *Truman Presidential Musem & Library*. www.trumanlibrary.org.

George Washington University, Meeting of the National Security Council, December 22, 1975. www.gwu.edu.

D.M. Giangreco and Robert E. Griffin, *Airbridge to Berlin—The Berlin Crisis of 1948, Its Origins and Aftermath*, Novato, CA: Presidio, 1988, as it appears at www.trumanlibrary.org.

HBC News, Joint Resolution of Congress, August 7, 1974. www.luminet.net.

George F. Kennan, Excerpts from Telegraphic Message from Moscow, February 22, 1946, *Vincent Ferraro's Home Page.* www.mtholyoke.edu.

——— (X), "The Sources of Soviet Conduct," *Foreign Affairs,* July 1947. http://darkwing.uoregon.edu.

John F. Kennedy, Broadcast to the American Public: July 25, 1961, *CNN.* www.cnn.com.

———, Letter to Chairman Nikita Khrushchev, October 22, 1961, *U.S. Department of State,* Vol. 11, Document no. 44. www.state.gov.

———, Speech Announcing the Quarantine Against Cuba, October 22, 1962, *Vincent Ferraro's Home Page.* www.mtholyoke.edu.

Robert F. Kennedy, in third oral history interview with John Barlow Martin, April 30, 1964, *Kennedy Assassination Homepage.* http://mcadams.posc.mu.edu.

Edward Lansdale, "Program Review [The Cuba Project]," February 20, 1962, *Parascope.com.* www.parascope.com.

George Marshall, Harvard University Address, June 5, 1947, *Radio Free Europe.* www.rferl.org.

National Security Council, Paper no. 68 (NSC-68), *Federation of American Scientists.* www.fas.org.

Donald Neff, "Nasser Comes to Power in Egypt, Frightening Britain, France and Israel," July 1996, *Washington Report on Middle East Affairs.* www.washington-report.org.

Richard Nixon, Speech on November 3, 1969, *Temple University OnLine Learning Program.* http://oll.temple.edu.

Alexander S. Payushkin, Letter to the U.S. Secretary of State, July 14, 1948, *Truman Library.* www.trumanlibrary.org.

Pink Noise Studios, Summary of the Report of the Independent Council. www.webcom.com.

Public Broadcasting System, "People and Events: The Berlin Blockade." www.pbs.org.

Ronald Reagan, 1985 State of the Union Address, *The Gipper.com.* www.thegipper.com.

Richard Reeves, "13 Days in October," *New York Times,* October 8, 1997. www.mtholyoke.edu.

Arthur Schlesinger Jr., Memorandum from the President's Special Assistant to President Kennedy, May 3, 1961, *U.S. Department of State,* Vol. 10, document no. 196. www.state.gov.

Harry S. Truman, Address Before a Joint Session of Congress, March 12, 1947, *Fletcher School of Law and Diplomacy.* www.tufts.edu.

U.S. Department of State, Telegram to U.S. Embassy in the Soviet Union, Vol. 11, Document no. 52, October 23, 1962. www.state.gov.

U.S. Department of State, Telegram from U.S. Embassy in the Soviet Union, Vol. 11, Document no. 48, October 23, 1962. www.state.gov.

U.S. Senate Committee on Foreign Relations, 90th Congress, 1st Session, *Vincent Ferraro's Home Page.* www.mtholyoke.edu.

Websites

American Civil Rights Review (http:// webusers.anet-stt.com). Contains information, links, and archived documents for a number of American Civil Rights movements, including the anti-war movement to protest Vietnam.

The Contemporary Portuguese Political History Research Centre's Website (www.cphrc.org.uk). Contains a number of documents on Portuguese history including the Alvor Agreement that granted independence to Angola.

Churchill Center and Societies' Winston Churchill Home Page (www.winston churchill.org). The site has a lot of information on Winston Churchill's life and career. It includes the transcripts of a number of his speeches.

Dwight D. Eisenhower Library at the University of Texas (www.eisenhower. utexas.edu). Contains a variety of information on Eisenhower's presidency including links to primary documents.

Fletcher School of Law Diplomacy Website (www.tufts.edu). Contains a library resources section that includes the "Multilaterals Project," an ongoing project to make the texts of a number of important documents available on the Web.

The Gipper.com (www.thegipper.com). This is a website dedicated to "advancing the Reagan Revolution." It contains transcripts of many of "the gipper's" speeches as well as news articles.

Kennedy Assassination Homepage (mcadams.posc.mu.edu). Provides an online collection of documents, interviews, information, and links to other websites about the Kennedy administration and assassination.

The Kimball Files (darkwing.uoregon. edu). University of Oregon professor Alan Kimball provides a number of primary documents online.

Professor James M. Lindsay's Home Page (www.uiowa.edu). Professor Lindsay has placed a number of primary documents on the Web.

Parascope.com (www.parascope.com). A website dedicated to uncovering government cover-ups. It contains documentary evidence on everything from covert operations to aliens.

Radio Free Europe (www.rferl.org). The website of Radio Free Europe contains a lot of news and analysis of current world affairs (from a U.S. government perspective). It also contains a few primary documents.

Reagan Foundation Website (www.reagan foundation.com). This official Ronald Reagan presidential website includes an archive of a number of Reagan's speeches that have been made available online.

U.S. Air Forces in Europe Berlin Airlift Website (www.usafe.af.mil). Contains a lot of useful facts, figures, and information on the Berlin Airlift.

U.S. State Department (www.state.gov). This is truly a historian's dream. Thousands of documents on foreign policy and governmental decisions.

Vincent Ferraro's Home Page (www. mtholyoke.edu). "Vinnie" is a professor at Mount Holyoke College who has created a website with links to hundreds of primary documents that are available on the Web. It includes a number of documents related to the Cold War and is one of the most fascinating and useful sites on the Web.

⋆ Index ⋆

☆ Picture Credits ☆

Cover Image: © Hulton Archive
Associated Press, AP, 35, 58, 68, 100, 105
© AFP/CORBIS, 41
© Bettmann/CORBIS, 24, 27, 37, 42, 48, 63, 91, 99
© Copley News Service, 109
© Digital Stock, 8
© Bill Gentile/CORBIS, 102
© Hulton Archive, 12, 17, 19, 23, 28, 29, 32, 49, 50, 53, 55, 60, 66, 68, 70, 73, 77, 79, 88, 89, 94, 97, 101
Library of Congress, 44, 46
National Archives, 15, 74, 76, 81, 83, 84
United Nations, 39

☆ About the Author ☆

Jennifer Keeley is a freelance writer and former teacher who lives and works in Seattle, Washington. She graduated from Carleton College in 1996 with a degree in history and her teaching certificate. She has taught history and social studies in both the Seattle and Minneapolis Public Schools.